I am Akbar Agha
Memories of the Afghan Jihad and the Taliban

First Draft Publishing/*Originals*

Sayyed Mohammad Akbar Agha: I am Akbar Agha
Memories of the Afghan Jihad and the Taliban
Anand Gopal: Foreword

Published in Germany in 2014 by First Draft Publishing GmbH,

ISBN 978-3-944214-09-2 *(softcover)*
ISBN 978-3-944214-08-5 *(kindle)*
ISBN 978-3-944214-10-8 *(epub)*

Cover Photography: © Philip Poupin
www.philippoupin.fr
Concept & Design: Bureau Christoph Dunst
www.christophdunst.com
Cover Design: Bureau Christoph Dunst
Typefaces: Heimat Mono *www.atlasfonts.com* & Arnhem
www.ourtype.be

First Draft Publishing GmbH, Berlin – printed in Germany.

www.firstdraft-publishing.com
info@firstdraft-publishing.com

Table of Contents

Anand Gopal: Foreword

Early one morning in May 1987, Soviet tanks rolled across the Zheray desert into the lush district of Arghandab to launch the last great offensive of the Soviet-Afghan war. The villages surrounding Kandahar city had steadily fallen to the Islamist insurgents in recent years, and a six thousand-man Soviet-Afghan force had mobilized to clear the area, comprised of Moscow's 70th Motorized Rifle Brigade alongside Afghan army units under the command of Ismat Muslim and Gen. Abdul Rashid Dostum. The troops were converging in a pincer movement on the village of Charqulba, a de facto mujahedeen headquarters on the Arghandab river's western bank.

Fighting from irrigation ditches, the mujahedeen were able to slow the Soviet advance, and tanks got bogged down in the dense patchwork of pomegranate groves and apple orchards. As one week turned to the next, Soviet and Afghan army casualties mounted. Air support plowed the area with ordnance, but the mujahedeen were able to survive by spending days on end in bunkers and irrigation ditches. The tanks retreated to the open desert, acting as rear artillery for the Democratic Republic of Afghanistan's (DRA) infantry, which pushed through the orchards on foot.

Neither side was able to dislodge the other, and the battle settled into a protracted, bloody routine. "The enemy would begin the morning with an aircraft and artillery bombardment from the south and southeast," said Akhtar Jan, a mujahedeen commander. "Usually, they would then send eight helicopter gunships to work over the area. Then, they would launch infantry attacks. The Mujahedeen would emerge from their bunkers, occupy fighting positions and wait for the approaching infantry [1]." Losses mounted on both sides. Soviet and DRA army morale

plummeted, and the mujahedeen food supplies dwindled.
Then, the Soviets made a tactical error. They began filtering in from the northwest of Charqulba, through the holy village of Jelahor, which had been emptied of people over the course of the war. And a second group pushed in from the opposite bank of the Arghandab river, through the village of Char Bagh, which was a base of poor religious students who had formed units of their own to fight the Russians. These students, called *taliban* in Pashto, had been among the earliest to take up arms against the Soviets. Akbar Agha was one of them.

The battle raged across multiple fronts, the Soviet-Afghan force pressing closer to Charqulba, the mujahedeen sneaking out at night to mine the road ahead of their advance. The sky thrummed incessantly, and Char Bagh was regularly in flames. On June 3rd, nearly two weeks into the fighting, a series of 122 mm Soviet Howitzer shells struck the main *taliban* base in the village, killing the legendary *taliban* commander Lala Malang—perhaps the most important mujahedeen leader in all of Kandahar. The news prompted *taliban* from around the province to descend upon Arghandab, sparking one of the most intense battles of the entire Soviet occupation. The fighting continued for weeks, and when it was over, hundreds of mujahedeen were dead. But they did not cede ground. In the face of such steadfast resistance, scores of Afghan army conscripts defected or simply threw their weapons in ditches and fled. On a July evening, after thirty-four days of fighting, Soviet forces abandoned Arghandab forever.

The Battle of Arghandab forms a central part of Kandahar lore, but you won't hear about it in most accounts of the Taliban movement. Instead, according to the well-known story, the Taliban arose in extremist madrassas in Pakistan, spread across war-weary Afghanistan in two short years, and imposed an alien theocracy on the population of the likes the world had never before seen. They were a phenomenon unprecedented in Afghan history, this story goes, a symptom of the hyper-regionalization of the conflict. Their ideological origins were rooted in prominent Pakistani madrassas and in an austere, imported brand of Islam called Deobandism. In Kandahar, though, you will hear a very different history. The origins of the Taliban, and indeed, the entire post-Soviet order in the province, lie in experiences like the Battle of Arghandab. They lie in the shared memories of suffering, bravery, and friendship, forged in the trenches of a cataclysmic upheaval that reverberates to this day. In recent years, a steady trickle of insider accounts of the Taliban have attempted to retrace this history, and by doing so challenge the prevailing story of the movement's origins. The seminal work in this genre is *My Life in the Taliban* by Mullah Abdul Salaam Zaeef. *I am Akbar Agha* follows in this tradition, presenting a detailed chronicle of the Taliban's beginnings, along with the unique perspective of someone who was ideologically aligned with the movement but remained independent during its years in power. In it, we find the most comprehensive look yet of the 1980s *taliban* fronts, autonomous bands of religious students who fought alongside the mainstream mujahedeen in the southern provinces of Kandahar, Helmand, and Zabul. His account, and others like it, show that today's Taliban is a homegrown phenomenon, with roots in these 1980s *taliban* fronts and antecedents dating back centuries. If we start from here, much of Afghan history over the past few decades begins to look different, and, I'd venture, more coherent.

Sayyed Muhammad Akbar Agha was born in the 1961 in Jelahor village of Arghandab. As home to Sayyeds, a tribe which, Afghans believe, consists of descendants of the Prophet Muhammad. This lent a scholarly and religious air to Jelahor, and for as long as anyone can remember, it has been one of the most prominent centers of spiritual instruction in southern Afghanistan. As a young *talib*, Akbar Agha took lessons from a number of scholars in the village. Unlike most future Taliban leaders, though, he continued his education in Pakistan, returning for the outbreak of jihad upon the Russian invasion. The experience abroad appears to have given him a less provincial outlook than other top Taliban figures, many of whom had never left greater Kandahar until capturing power in the 1990s.

True to the Afghan form of storytelling, the history Akbar Agha recounts here is a pastiche of tense stand-offs, daring escapes, and battlefield miracles. There is little attempt to thread a linear narrative, illustrating the way the war is remembered and spoken of today. So it may be helpful to trace the outlines of the jihad in Kandahar: the first-anti-government activity began following the Communist coup in 1978, largely due to imprisonment and torture of landed and religious elites. But full-blown insurrection took place only after the Soviet invasion of 1979.

In the early years, there were eight mujahedeen parties in Kandahar: the seven official, Pakistan-sanctioned organizations and Fedayeen-i-Islam, a Salafist-inspired outfit based in Spin Boldak under the command of Ismat Muslim.

Around this time, religious students in Zabul province began forming autonomous groups, and the phenomenon quickly spread to Kandahar and Helmand. Often, these groups were tied to particular areas and so came to be called "fronts"—the Nagehan front, the Tur Taaq front, the Pashmol front, and so on. With the patrimonial structure of the jihad, though, in time certain commanders became associated with fronts, and so, confusingly, there are also fronts named after individuals or even institutions. A *talib* could switch fronts, and indeed, this happened often, creating a regularly morphing *taliban* network.

The *taliban* fronts were nominally aligned to one of eight mujahedeen groups; many of the Arghandab fronts initially had ties with Fedayeen-i-Islam, until its commander Ismat Muslim switched sides and joined the Communists in 1984.

Though the *taliban* fronts were, by most accounts, appreciated and respected in Kandahari society, they were not a significant military force on the battlefield—if only because the bulk of funding and weapons went to the official parties. Akbar Agha's account, however, is told almost entirely from within the perspective of these fronts—with only rare mentions of "non-*talib*" mujahedeen—which gives a sense of just how insular the *talib*'s world was.

In the jihad's early years, the two sides battled to a stalemate, but an influx of US funding and weapons after 1984 began to turn the tide. In Kandahar, there was little linking a commander to one of the seven Pakistan-based parties except for the availability of these weapons. As a consequence, whenever arms flowed changed course, mujahedeen units would shift alliances accordingly. The funding increase of those years sparked a battlefield restructuring as many groups, including *talibs*, switched from Harakat-i-Islami to Hizb-i-Islami Khalis. By 1986, the US was supplying stinger missiles and upped funding to unprecedented numbers. Insurgents were now able to temporarily overrun government bases and district centers, setting the stage for the pivotal 1987 Battle of Arghandab.

Arghandab had all the makings of a insurgent stronghold: its dense pomegranate groves provided ample cover for guerrilla ambushes, its proximity to government-controlled Kandahar city allowed for frequent raids, and its charismatic mujahedeen leaders, such as the colorful Mullah Naqib and the intrepid Lala Malang, made for easy recruitment. The Arghandab river, which gives the district its name, bisects the area into sociologically distinct halves. The eastern bank has the choice land, in part because of a large canal, and is populated by the Alikozai tribe. Historically, this area was more integrated into the central state, with Alizozais forming part of the tribal aristocracy that has ruled Kandahar for generations. The western bank, which abuts the Zheray desert, is poorly irrigated. Here, the population is mixed between Alikozais and a number of tribes of lesser political importance. After 1979, many of the tribal elite from the eastern bank fled to Pakistan, leaving a vacuum of political power which lowly mullahs and impoverished religious students from the western bank soon filled. Then, as today, most fighting took place on the western bank, while the eastern shore functioned as rebel redoubt and civilian zone.

Akbar Agha fought in a series of *taliban* fronts around Arghandab and west of Kandahar city, in villages like Pashmol. Many of the individuals he describes fighting alongside would later become leading members of the Taliban government and the anti-American insurgency. When the Taliban movement emerged in 1994 to sweep through the south, Akbar Agha remained on the sidelines; his intimate knowledge of the leadership together with his position outside the organization make him unique in this regard, and here he offers intriguing criticisms of the 1990s regime.

In 2004, Akbar Agha launched an anti-American insurgent group called Jaish ul-Muslimeen, which denounced Taliban leader Mullah Muhammad Omar and called for a break with the old guard Taliban. The group kidnapped three foreign United Nations workers, demanding a ransom and the release of Taliban prisoners. After negotiations, the three were returned unharmed, and Akbar Agha was quickly apprehended by Pakistan and handed over to Afghan security. Akbar Agha claims that members of his group had acted without his imprimatur, whereas the Afghan government alleges that he in fact masterminded the whole affair.

In 2008, I visited Akbar Agha in prison a number of times. I didn't get any closer to the truth of the matter, but I was struck by how well connected he remained to Taliban leaders. He was released in 2010, and recently formed a new group, Khlasoon Lar, ('The Salvation Path') aimed at promoting peace talks between the Taliban and the Afghan government.

An eventual peace and reconciliation process will need to help Afghans come to terms with the type of history contained in these pages. The fragmentation of Afghanistan over the past three decades has meant the fragmentation of its memories, too. There are certain prevailing narratives about the course of these wars, but there are other, equally important, stories that deserve to be told: the Kandahar jihad, the brutal civil war in Kabul and elsewhere, the great suffering of northern communities at the hands of the Taliban, the continuing suffering of rural southern communities by all sides. Akbar Agha's book is an important step in this direction.

Anand Gopal
New York, June 2014

I am Akbar Agha

Preface

Praise be to Allah and peace be up on Mohammad, his family and all his companions.
It is obvious that a bloody war has been raging in Afghanistan for the past thirty-five years. This has left not hi ng but fear, pain, horror, and tiresome human and financial loss for all Afghans. The invasion of the Red army was the start of this war. At the same time, Allah allowed Afghans to perform an important religious obligation, holy jihad. After putting up with many problems, wounds, imprisonment, emigrations and martyrdom, Afghans were awarded a great blessing with the help of God. This verse of the sweet Qur'an confirms this issue: "You may dislike something, but in fact that thing is good for you".
Afghans defeated the biggest invading power of the time and achieved a great victory in the region and in the world. Once again, the Afghans' zeal, faithfulness and heroism was a reminder to the foreigners that this Muslim and Mujahed nation would not bow its head to anyone and that it would not tolerate invasion of its religion, homeland and territory. Note, too, that by doing so Afghans liberated the other nations of the surrounding region as well as their own homeland.

Unfortunately, instead of making up for the past destruction and thanking Allah for this great blessing and happiness, Afghans turned to conflict amongst themselves seeking power. They did not raise themselves to the verse of the Qur'an which states: "If you thank for what you have, we will give you more." Civil war, theft and several other vices reached a point that was no longer tolerable for the people. This was the time when the Taliban decided to rescue the country from the ongoing abhorrence. The Taliban were warmly welcomed by the public and their support and movement reached every corner of the country very quickly. They decommissioned many armed groups after capturing Kabul and established a powerful central government after a long period of war in the country. This turned out to be unacceptable to our neighbours and the Westerners, so once again they invaded this soil after implementing some cunning plans.

Today, many writers have written about Afghanistan's condition: war, the foreign invasions, domestic problems, their causes and the proposed solutions. From my point of view, the veracity and soundness of these reports cannot be fully trusted. Most of these just quoted from the media or other news sources, and others were just based on quotes from some individuals, very few of whom were reliable. Some reports were biased and sometimes the writer was himself from one of the parties involved. As a consequence, following encouragement by jihadi and other friends, as a Muslim Afghan Mujahid, I have decided to put in words what I have seen during this time. This book that you have in your hands includes incidents from the beginning of the jihad together with reflections on that which I have personally witnessed. It covers the beginning of the holy jihad, the time of the holy jihad, the fall of the Russians and their puppet government, the defamation of jihad and the mujahedeen and the beginnings of the public hate against them, internal and foreign conspiracies and different plots against Islam and Afghanistan, as well as answering the following questions: Who were the Taliban? What happened to them and me after their period of rule? What was the result of the jihad? I also speak about my arrest by the Pakistani government, their ill treatment of me and the rest of the detainees. My handing over to the Americans and bitter memories of the five-year imprisonment are events that have filled the upcoming pages. Many of my friends wanted me to shed light on how the Americans treated the detainees. For this reason, I deemed it appropriate to begin with my memories of the Islamic jihad and then write about my imprisonment and suffering.

The only purpose of mine behind writing down these memories is to provide information for the next generation (especially the youth) so they will become aware of not only my memories but also the virtue, heroism and suffering of the entire Afghan

Mujahid nation. At the end, I once again send peace to Mohammad and praise his family and companions; I am grateful to Allah, who privileged a small creature like me with the holy jihad, and who kept me away from civil war, and who soundly got me out of many troubling imprisonments.

Brief Introduction

After praising Allah, sending peace to the Prophet and expressing my gratefulness, I introduce myself:
I am Sayyed Mohammad Akbar Agha, son of Mawlawi Amir Mohammad Agha, grandson of Sayyed Sher Mohammad Agha and great grandson of Sayyed Ahmad Gul Sahebzada. I am from the tribe of the Sadat[2], and from that, the Yasinzai branch. I was born in Juy Lahore village of Arghandab district of Kandahar province in 1340 (1961). I carried out my primary schooling with my father, who was known as Little Hajji Agha, and Agha Mawlana Abdul Hamid, who was knowns as Big Hajji Agha. They were both great clerics who had trained my Talibs. Due to their passion for education, a madrassa called Hamidiyya Hashimiyya was built in the Surkhab refugee camp in Pakistan with great efforts from these two clerics. After setting it up, they trained many Talibs who presented several other clerics to the community after spreading out to other madrassas in Peshawar and Karachi. Thanks to their presence, our village was known as the village of the ulemaa'.

After this primary schooling, I studied for almost four and a half years with Mawlawi Akhtar Mohammad Agha and the martyred Mawlawi Serajuddin, both of whom were my father's students. After that I studied various religious subjects with Mawlana Abdul Haq at the Haqqania Madrassa in Akora Khattak. I also studied with Mawlana Abdul Halim at Sadr ul-Madaris, Mawlana Sami ul-Haq, Mufti Farid ur-Rahman, Mawlawi Fazal Mawla, Maghfurullah and some other teachers.
I studied the hadiths for a short period at Akora Khattak, but then for a longer period after the holy Jihad was finished. That second time I studied with Sheikh ul-Hadith Mawlana Muta-

wakkil Shah. I also taught for a short period of time in my village. My grandparents had come to Afghanistan from Bukhara. Four brothers of the Sayyed tribe migrated to the Pashin area of Baluchistan. These four brothers were Jamaluddin[3], Kamaluddin[4], Bilaluddin[5] and Jalaluddin[6]. The eldest brother (Jalaluddin) had four sons: Shadi, Haider, Mantar and Ismail. Shadi had two sons whose names were Yasin and Yousuf. Shadi and his eldest son (Yasin) are both buried in Zhranda area, just a kilometre away from Baluchistan shrine. One of the children of Yasin was called Mehter Musa, and he was buried in the Chola area of Muqur.

Sayyed Ahmed Gul Sahebzada was the son of Mehter Musa. He travelled during the summer and winter. He lived in Eesakhil area of Miyanwali Zela at the side of Kurma Road. He came to Ghazni province (Afghanistan) through Panyali and Gumal Tank of Dera Ismael Khan. Khan Bahadur, a resident of Panyali (Dera Ismael Khan), gave them some land so they would not have to be on the move all the time. The current Yasinzai institution was built on that land.

Ahmed Gul Sahebzada had nine sons, all of whom took religious studies classes and became ulemaa'. There was Sayyed Abdul Halim[7], Sayyed Din Mohammad, Sayyed Noor Mohammad, Shah Abdul Aziz and Sayyed Abdul Hakim. These five all settled in Penyala. The remaining four — Sayyed Shir Mohammad, Sayyed Pir Mohammad, Sayyed Abdul Ghaffar and Sayyed Abdul Sattar — came to Kandahar. The governor of Kandahar at the time — Amir Mohammad Osman — gave them 1600 acres of land in Jelahor (Arghandab district), and 200 families of their relatives settled in this part of Kandahar.

I am Akbar Agha/Memories of the Afghan Jihad and the Taliban

THE START OF THE HOLY JIHAD

The communist regime led by Noor Mohammad Taraki was established in the month of Saur 1357 (1978) as the result of an awful coup that had the obvious support of the Russians. This really was the beginning of the destruction of Afghanistan, the start of our problems and misfortune. The faithless communist belief — in contradiction to the lofty values of Islam and which could not be implemented in our Muslim society — was unacceptable to our Muslim nation. They impudently wanted to implement and impose the awful Marxism and the communist rules of their red overlords on our country. They wanted to do this by putting oppressed Afghans in trouble, by imprisoning them, by killing them en masse, by destroying their villages and homes and by forcing them to flee. In such a dark moment, ulemaa' issued fatwas for jihad and the Afghan nation declared a jihad against them. I was studying at a madrassa at the time. It coincided with the moment when the Islamic movement had mobilised for jihad against the puppet regime. A short while later, this movement split into two parties — *Hizb-e Islami* and Jamiat-e Islami. At the same time, ulemaa' from all over the country set up the Harakat-e Inqelab-e Islami, under the leadership of Mawlawi Mohammad Nabi Mohammadi, to perform jihad against the invading army and its puppet regime.

... THE HAQQANIA MADRASSA

I was studying at the Haqqania madrassa at the time. When Mawlawi Rahimullah Zurmati and Mawlawi Abdul Sattar Seddiqi came to visit, we decided to perform jihad as well. We

moved swiftly towards Miranshah. We received some military training under Wahidyar's supervision [8]. We then returned to Quetta. At this point the office of the Harakat-e Inqelab-e Islami was headed by Noor Ahmad Shah Agha and had newly opened in Quetta. The armed jihad hadn't started in Kandahar yet.
When our trained group arrived in Kandahar, we began our jihad under the leadership of Mawlawi Akhtar Mohammad Agha. We answered the call of jihad coming from Kandahar, Helmand, Farah, Nimruz, Uruzgan and up to Herat. The public didn't hesitate to provide financial or manpower assistance to the mujahedeen. With the money we raised, we bought sixty poor-quality weapons from Adamkhil area of Peshawar. We also bought a few Iranian Shaldazi guns, the magazines of which can hold twenty bullets. They were considered good weapons at the time.
Before I begin the discussion of my jihadi operations, I should mention that my jihad was carried out with the fronts whose members were all Talibs. I was a Talib myself, and the Taliban movement was eventually established from those fronts. The Taliban movement were mostly former mujahedeen, therefore, and not a gathering together of new religious students.

THE TALIBAN MOVE AGAINST THE RUSSIANS

I would also like to mention some other points.

1. The leaders of the Taliban (Mullah Omar's Taliban) were mostly mujahedeen of the jihadi fronts.
2. Talibs were the ones who first started the jihad in the southwest.
3. I will make some points about the organised Taliban fronts in order to show why Talibs stood up against vice and devilishness in Kandahar.

Talibs were the ones who began the jihad in most provinces, especially Kandahar. For instance, the heads of our front in Tur Taaq were Talibs and most of the mujahedeen as well.
Our front in Nagehan — which was made up of Talibs — was the second biggest after the Tur Taaq front. Then there was a Talib front named after the martyred Qari Azizullah, and then there was Hafiz Abdul Karim's Taliban front. Similarly, there was Mullah Musa Kalim's Taliban front in Zabul, and in Hel-

mand there were the two Taliban fronts of Ra'ees Mullah Abdul Wahid and Mohammad Nasim Akhundzada.
Our front was initially called Al-Seria al-Farooqia, Mullah Hajji Mohammad Akhund's front was called 'Haqqania', and Mawlawi Akhtar Mohammad Agha's front was called Al-Najia. There were also fronts led by Mullah Shireen Akhund, Commander Abdul Raziq, Mullah Mohammad Sadiq and Faizullah Akhundzada. The Taliban government was created from these fronts. These fronts were united and agreed with each other. Most operations were put to a vote and only took place following the assent of all of these fronts. The fact that there were joint groups on operations was a sign of their unity.

There was one joint group in Mahalajat which remained there for years and was lead by Mullah Burjan for most of the time. The group was there to assist the Mahalajat mujahedeen. Another could be found in Abbasabad (behind the prison).
Whenever mujahedeen in Arghandab or any other area got into trouble, our joint group was sent to that area.
We had courts, too, and all the fronts supported the decisions taken there. The courts implemented *huduud* and *qisas* with this power.
There were some other public non-Talib fronts, but they followed the lead of the Talib fronts. Afghan and Pakistani Talibs would come over to Afghanistan from the Pakistani madrassas for their holidays or when the mujahedeen were under pressure. Their fronts had sections that were devoted to the duty of Amr bil Maroof wa Nahi min al-Munkar[9]. They didn't permit the use of *naswar*[10], for example, or cigarettes on their fronts. They carried out their operations in an organised manner following consultation with all parties. They avoided fights among other Muslim groups and encouraged jihad against the Russians. The mujahedeen belonging to these fronts later became the leaders of the Taliban movement.

THE TUR TAAQ FRONT, THE TALIBAN'S FIRST BATTLE AND DEFEAT

The mujahedeen thought that 'Tur Taaq', the name of a well-known mountain near Pashmol, would be a good place to set up their front. A base was established there. Expenses and food for the front were provided by the public; most of our supplies were sent from our villages. Mujahedeen came from many different places to join the front. The youth from remote areas gathered together like butterflies with great jihadi enthusiasm. The front gradually started to come together. Unfortunately, we didn't have many weapons, and even the ones we had weren't a match for the modern weaponry — especially the tanks and war planes — of the enemy. At that time, the mujahedeen weren't familiar with the tactics, strategy and tricks of war that the ten years struggle would teach us.

The Russian red army moved on Tur Taaq, heavily bombing and shelling the mujahedeen base with tanks and artillery. Many of our mujahedeen were martyred and wounded in the face of so much Russian bombing and shelling. The mujahedeen were able to stand firm against a great deal of hardship, but couldn't hold the base. Those who survived scattered away to many different places until a bigger front was prepared — and with it, a bigger battle. I returned to my village and to my home. Our life had become tough, and our house had been searched by the puppets (Afghan government soliders or police cooperating with the Soviets) several times. Finally, we were forced to leave. In 1979, together with the martyred Lala Malang and Amir Mohammad Agha, I received training in how to fire an RPG. We opened a front that was officially registered with the Harakat-e Enqelab party. At that time, there were no other fronts (other than that of Esmat Muslim) in the area. There was a second front led by Mawlawi Akhtar Mohammad Agha. Among the hundred or so people who joined up with this front were the martyred Lala Malang (son of Mawlawi Sadozai Agha), Sayyed Amir Mohammad Agha (who later became influential during the Taliban time), as well as the popular Kandahari wrestlers Aminullah Pahlawan and Hajji Sardar Pahlawan (who were martyred in a battle against the occupying army in Registan). The party gave us thirty weapons, and one RPG and a heavy machine gun.

THE JIHAD AND THE MIRACLE OF THE MUJAHEDEEN

When our small group of mujahedeen decided to move towards Afghanistan, we departed early in the morning from Quetta to Dalbandin. From there, we headed towards Registan. The way to Registan was extremely tough and the weather was still very hot. There was a river at the Naru area near a hill that seemed to be a likely place for planes to bombard.

The mujahedeen caravan stopped there to take a break. The water from the river was bitter tasting; this is something the people of that area had known for years. But the heat, the long route and exhaustion forced the mujahedeen to decide to drink the bitter water. When we drew some of the water, by the power of Allah it had miraculously turned sweet. This was clearly a miracle of holy intention, firm faith and the sacrifice of the mujahedeen. This incident was very similar to something that happened to the Prophet Joseph (PBUH) who, when he fell into a well with bitter and putrid water, found that it had turned sweet through Allah'swill. This is something that has remained in my memory.

The mujahedeen stayed at Naru region for two months. Those two months were filled with problems, hunger and thirst. Our affiliate political party — Harakat-e Enqelab — sent 100 weapons, three RPG launchers, and a heavy machine gun. Also, with the help of our friends, we bought 20 Iranian weapons whose magazines held 20 bullets. After a long break, we moved towards Helmand and stayed in the forest near the area called Falalki. It was a good place to hide. We brought five cars and some other important equipment to the other side of the Helmand river. After walking for a whole night, we arrived in Musa Qala.

TALIB MUJAHEDEEN FACING THE RED ARMIES

It was dark and silent and the mujahedeen caravan was moving forward. We arrived in a village called Shaban at dawn. The mujahedeen hadn't even put down their packs when the helicopters and jet planes of the Red Army appeared in the sky. They heavily bombarded our caravan. The helicopters shot at the mujahedeen with heavy machine guns and we also faced artillery fire. One of the cars was set on fire and all the mujahedeen inside were martyred. A bomb hit the second car as well, but only the old grey-bearded driver — a dedicated mujahed man — was martyred. A few of the other mujahedeen were wounded. We received some help from the people of Shaban area, which was greatly appreciated. They helped us move our cars and other equipment. Finally, the mujahedeen caravan reached Musa Qala. This was the seventh day following the capturing of Musa Qala, where Mullah Mohammad Nasim Akhundzada was leading the mujahedeen. News spread that a large military force of the Red Army was approaching Musa Qala. Mullah Mohammad Nasim Akhundzada asked for our assistance. We remained there for a few days before deciding to move on. We lent a heavy machine gun to Mullah Mohammad Nasim Akhundzada before we left.

WHERE DID THE MUJAHEDEEN FROM OUR FRONT GO TO FROM MUSA QALA?

After we left Musa Qala, we reached an area of Sangin district called Fadai, a place where there are many tall trees. This was believed to be a good hiding place, out of sight of the Red Army war planes. Also it's worth mentioning that the people of Sangin were extremely hospitable. After a short stay, we decided to return to the Tur Taaq Front, where we had fought the big battle the previous year. We sent our car back to Quetta along with a number of mujahedeen.

We didn't have our own vehicles, so we made our way in cars rented from people in Sangin district. We arrived in Tur Taaq after a long journey. From the moment we arrived, we didn't have food or any other necessary items. The residents of the villages near and far had left on account of the war, and there was nobody to help the mujahedeen. We used to heat up the leftover dried bread from the previous year on a fire made of thorn bushes. That is what we ate. We heard that our mujahedeen had run into Red Army tanks on their way back to Quetta and had been martyred and injured. A few of our cars had been burnt up. We discussed the situation of our fellow mujahedeen. We wanted to get them out of this bad situation. Nuruddin and I were selected as leaders and decided to supply food and other necessary equipment from the houses and from our village in Arghandab. The mujahedeen were starving by this point, and it was necessary to get ready for the upcoming battle. We left — Nuruddin, myself and a few other mujahedeen — for Arghandab. On the way, we passed Baluch House. Someone called Jilani Baluch helped us and found a way for us to move on to Arghandab in the morning. Finally we reached Jelahor with much joy the next day still carrying our weapons. The puppet government soldiers were crawling all over the place.

We collected food and some other necessities before returning to the Tur Taaq front. We arrived at Tur Taaq after a long and tiring walk, albeit with the peace of mind that came from finally having the necessary food and other supplies to keep us going for a while.

HOW DID WE GO TO NAGEHAN AND WHO HAD INVITED US?

Some of our friends said that we should travel to Pashmol to fight. Others thought it would be better to go to Arghandab because some in the Nagehan area of Arghandab had taken up opposition against the puppet government. It was more likely that there would be fighting there than in Pashmol.

We talked it through with elders and representatives from Nagehan and learnt that they wanted us to set up a base for them. That area was full of government forces and communist elements, so opportunities for jihad were restricted. We accepted the invitation, nevertheless, and some two hundred mujahedeen travelled to Nagehan. We set up a base there and appointed various section heads to organise ourselves and to serve the people in a better manner. A court, a prison and a weapons cache were all established. We tried the criminals of the homeland in our court alongside the traitors. If someone was on trial, we put them in jail.

Slowly the base became more and more powerful. Well-known mujahedeen from the surrounding areas joined up with us. Among these were Mullah Naqibullah Akhund, Mullah Mohammad Ismaeel Akhund, Mullah Nuruddin Turabi and Mawlawi Abdur Razzaq. We came up with operations against the Red Army and its slaves from time to time. Sometimes we came out onto the paved road to search vehicles and to arrest any communists we were able to find. Sometimes we carried out ambushes at the two-way intersection at Shah Agha, near Nazarjan Bagh/Garden. Many tanks, artillery transport vehicles and other military equipment were burnt on this way, and many soldiers and military personnel were killed. We inflicted heavy losses on them in short a short tie, and also captured many weapons in booty during these attacks.

As a result of the unlimited enthusiasm and love of the public for the jihad and the mujahedeen, all our financial expenses were provided by ordinary local people. We were even able to purchase weapons and ammunition out of the money donated by the public. In short, the mujahedeen became very powerful in a short time, and we were able to clear the area from the puppets. Successive defeats of the puppet government forces and attacks on the Red Army convoys forced the government to prepare a heavy attack.

THE RED ARMY, THE PUPPET GOVERNMENT'S BIG MILITARY FORCE, AND ENCIRCLING NAGEHAN

The Russians prepared a large force with the help of the communist regime and moved on Nagehan. They encircled the whole area upon arriving there. Kandahar Silo (the bread baking company) was near to Nagehan and it was chosen as the command centre of the occupying forces. They began a heavy bombardment of the area from the air, in addition to mortar and artillery fire. Early in the morning, their infantry forces started to move in.

The mujahedeen had not faced such a serious fight before, having mostly carried out guerrilla attacks. We weren't familiar with the fighting techniques needed for such a large battle. Many Russians were killed and many tanks and military vehicles were burned in this large battle. At the same time, mujahedeen were dying and getting wounded. Mullah Mohammad Qasim from Shawhin, Mohammad Hashin Agha from Jelahor, Mullah Nazar Mohammad Akhund from Farah and many other mujahedeen were martyred in this battle.

The mujahedeen captured many weapons from the battle, however, and by late afternoon we had secured a victory. The Russian forces had been defeated by the power of Allah. The mujahedeen buried their martyrs and the wounded were treated. This four-day battle had caused much destruction. We assumed that the Russians would return to extract revenge, and we assumed correctly. Only four days passed before they returned with an even bigger force. They surrounded Nagehan and the neighbouring areas. Jet planes bombed us and mortars and artillery fire struck all around. Light and heavy weapons fire could be heard from all directions and the battle became fiercer and fiercer. By the late afternoon, the battle really had picked up pace and the Russians intensified their air strikes, tanks and infantry assault on the ground. We managed to hit nine tanks and burnt them down. This was the first time in Kandahar that that many tanks had been destroyed by the mujahedeen. The Russians and the government suffered greatly in that battle. In addition to the tanks just mentioned, many military vehicles had either been burnt down or were taken as booty by the mujahedeen. It was evening by the time the remaining occupying and puppet forces fled from the battlefield. The butterflies of almighty Allah's religion were victorious. The mujahedeen were successful.

Once again the Russians had suffered many casualties and significant material damages. Mujahedeen had been martyred and wounded. In general, however, this battle boosted the mujahedeen morale and their conviction grew stronger. This was the first time the Russians and the puppet government had to face that much damaged on the battlefield. It was the first time the mujahedeen had been able to shoot at the Russian helicopters, adding to our war experience and achievements. We saw things we hadn't seen before. Once again we saw the miracles of the mujahedeen and the martyrs, something witnessed by all. The miracle was that candles would burn at night over the graves of the martyrs from the first and second battle, but when the Russian forces would approach the graves, they wouldn't see anything there. The fresh shrines of the new martyrs had all sorts of powers at night. The battle had left behind so much damage and so many casualties, though. The village was a ruin and destruction was all around.

THE INTENTION TO LEAVE

Some twenty-five days after the Nagehan battle, the infidel government and its Red invading allies prepared themselves for a huge battle. They gathered soldiers, tanks, artillery, military vehicles and ammunition from the close and remote provinces. Not only in Nagehan, but in the entire Arghandab and Charbagh areas, they started operations. In addition to these operations, they were brutally searching people's houses. They were making the lives of the people very difficult, beating them up, looting their property and even killing their animals. These horrific actions spread fear and terror among the public, especially among the women and children. Barbarism and murder spread across the area. The Russians even killed chickens or animals they found in the houses. Outlying villages were bulldozed by tanks and the defenceless women, children and elders became trapped in blood and rubble.

The battle raged for a few nights. The mujahedeen fought with great faith and bravery. The ongoing shortage of ammunition and weapons was a real weakness, though. The mujahedeen parties couldn't deliver military supplies at such short notice and in such situation. Most of what we had access to had been used in the previous battles. The mujahedeen were in an extremely bad situation. Many children were martyred. There was no medicine or place to treat the injured. We didn't have any food and the public was under pressure from the Russians not to help us. We needed to release them from this hardship so we decided to leave Nagehan and retreat to a place of safety where we could treat our injured and get some weapons and ammunition supplies as well.

We left Nagehan at night. Nobody seemed to think about the injured at the time. Given the lack of weapons and ammunition we were all just trying to get to a safe location as soon as possible. There were two other mujahedeen with me. I was trying my best, however, to save the lives of the injured, to get them to a place where they could be treated. A few donkeys were being used to carry some ten injured men. With great bravery, we smashed our way out through Charbagh and through the Red Army soldiers. Then we went to the houses of Hajji Nek Mohammad, Hajji Abdul Aziz, Mohammad Naseem and Mohammad Omar Jan near Sarpoza at Mullah Saheb Dad Akhund Ghondai area. In such an atmosphere of fear, we were happy to reach the area. It was a safe place for the mujahedeen and our injured, and they didn't spare any effort in helping us. They brought some medicine from Pir Paimal Puza for the injured along with some good doctors. After eight days, the injured had started to recover. After their relative improvement, they helped us to secretly enter the city. This was what the tumultuous Saur revolution brought for the people of Afghanistan. The wild communists wanted to impose their hollow Marxist ideals upon us Afghans. It was an intolerable situation. People were forced to leave their villages and homes and flee without anything to a foreign country. When the Red Army took control of the area north of the Arghandab river, they stayed there for a long time; people were forced to flee because of their savage actions.

The mujahedeen also deemed it appropriate to leave the homeland in order to organise and continue the jihad in a better manner from across the border. Our village was full of people and there were some great mujahedeen fighters there who were all united. The front I mentioned above was being led from this place, so they were also forced to leave along with the rest of the people. At this point, we weren't sure what was happening to our home, we were young men and loved jihad. We were too busy with jihad to think about our houses and villages. We had a large portion of farming land and thanks to Allah's blessings we didn't face financial problems. That said, I had not been paying much attention to our own situation while I was fighting, so when I came home I found it vacant with not a soul to be found. This first time, seeing it in such a fearsome condition, I was brought to tears. It is true that loving the homeland is a part of the faith. And it is true that the separation from the homeland and one's relatives in such a crisis required great patience. But the rewards from Allah for putting up with such a situation also shouldn't be forgotten.

Our family and the other villagers travelled with great difficulty, reaching Quetta facing a great many problems and hardship. I should mention that the condition of the refugees got better with the support of Muslims from around the world as time passed. They were provided with education and health facilities. The mujahedeen and refugees gained high levels of education in all fields. In addition to gaining knowledge in social and political affairs, they became known among regional Islamic countries as well as at the international community. More importantly, Afghans fulfilled Allahs's great obligation, which is to say, the jihad. This has been exercised very rarely in the current times. Afghans gained this great achievement and gained honour from it.

THE TALIBAN'S SMALL GUERRILLA FIGHTS IN THE CITY AFTER THE NAGEHAN-ARGHANDAB BATTLE

After we left the area around Nagehan, we went to the city with the rest of the mujahedeen. I stayed with the Mullah of a mosque near Manzil Bagh known as Mawlawi Nasir Jami mosque. I knew the Mullah from before and started to collect support from the public to help the mujahedeen front. After this collection, we bought weapons, ammunition and other equipment. As time passed, other mujahedeen came to the city as well, figures such as Mullah Nuruddin Turabi, Mullah Habibullah Hanafi, Mullah Akhtar Mohammad Shali and Lala Malang. After some meetings, we agreed to form a new guerrilla group. We would conduct planned guerrilla attacks and help in providing supplies. Men and women from the area helped us in performing this holy religious duty.

A STRANGE INCIDENT

One day, our leader, Mawlawi Mohammad Akhtar Agha, told me to bring some ammunition to a mujahedeen group based in Charbagh. The ammunition and bullets had been placed at Mawlawi Serajuddin castle located near the Kabul Darwaza area. I went with a few other mujahedeen and brought six or seven hundred bullets from the safe location. Nuruddin Turabi travelled a little bit ahead of us on a bicycle, scouting ahead. He would turn back if he came across any Russians or puppet government members. If not, we would follow behind him with the bullets hidden in our motorbikes.

Turabi had unexpectedly and unnoticed by us stopped along the way to talk to someone. We thought he had gone on so assumed there were no problems on the way. When I reached Kabul Darwaza I noticed that the puppet government officials were carrying out searches. Turabi arrived a little after me, also noting the situation. I tried to turn back but they noticed and shouted at me to stop. When I kept going, they shot at me with an AK-47. I accelerated away on my motorbike and took the sub-road west. The bullets hit the front of my bike. Soon after I entered Jan Mohammad Ustad's home. The infidels were chasing me, but there were only women in Jan Mohammad Ustad's house. One woman called Murakai, who was very brave, called on the other women to help. They put the bullets in small barrels and let them down in the well. They gave me some of their boys' clothes so as not to be recognised. I was still changing into them when the infidel soldiers arrived and started shouting. Murakai told them that she could not open the gate of the castle. They insisted that they must search the house, however. Murakai stood fast and refused to open it.

We decided that I should leave the house and asked the women about our options. It turns out there was a roof through which I could escape to the neighbour's house. In this way, Allah saved us. This was a time when Afghans — men and women — would help the mujahedeen by every effort possible. Another friend of ours, Niaz Mohammad, went to the house later that afternoon and retrieved the bullets from the well and brought them to us. After we left Nagehan, the mujahedeen were divided into small groups, but the area of our operations expanded. Some groups planned and conducted small guerrilla operations inside the city, while others would ambush the Red Army convoys on the Kandahar-Herat highway. This method was highly effective, so the mujahedeen achieved several victories in short order with the help of almighty Allah.

MY ARREST AND QUICK RELEASE

I was busy performing jihad as part of a guerrilla group inside the city. Abdul Rahman Shah Agha, a well-known figure in Kandahar, had given me a Mercedes Benz car. I intended to visit my family, having not seen them for a long time, ever since they left our village. I headed to our meeting point, the Mawlawi Nasir Jami big mosque. I noticed that Nuruddin Turabi and some other men had reached the area just before me. They first had waited for me, but then had gone on their own. I asked for the car to Quetta.

It was obvious that the puppet government's intelligence services were tracking me. Half an hour after I arrived at the mosque, around 35 puppet government officials arrived and entered the mosque brusquely. It was clear from how they were behaving that they were drunk. They came up to the room where I was sitting, and when they entered they beat me severely, as if they had finally found the person who had killed their entire family. Some of them punched me and kicked me, others stamped on my chest with their hard military boots, while others hit me on my head and my back.

When the AK-47 butts had turned red with the blood from my head and body and when the ruthless predators had grown tired, they calmed down, tied my hands and feet and started searching me. They found some 'night letters' and two pistols — a German Walter pistol and a Russian TT. Once again they beat me very severely. They became so angry that I thought they would kill me then and there. They pulled me out by my legs and hands and threw me on the ground near the room in the mosque where they had found the letters and the pistols.

I grew dizzy with the pain and thought they had broken my back. The governor of the time, Engineer Zarif, had ordered the death of any mujahed found with government-issued weapons. This, he said, was because the seizure of a government-issued weapon means that you had killed a government employee and taken the weapon as booty. One of the men loaded his AK-47 and pointed it at me. Suddenly, the other infidels shouted out to stop him; they suggested that if I was kept alive, I might be able to help them locate some of my friends. Four of them took me into a military jeep after untying my feet. The rest remained at the mosque.

On the way, any time we ran into an adult man with a beard they would ask me if I knew him. When I told them 'no', they would punch me. The vehicle sped off in the direction of the road leading to Kabul. I made up my mind to throw myself out of the vehicle at an appropriate point so as to satisfy my thirst for martyrdom and to retain all the information I had about the mujahedeen. I was afraid I would be forced to give up some information if I was tortured. I was still thinking about these things when we arrived at Deh Khwaja.

The driver slowed down, turning at the recently paved road (then a dirt track) near to Zhir school. We parked near Hajji Lalak Mama mosque on the other side of the road. They used to call the mujahedeen the 'English' back then. They talked among themselves and said they should go to the mosque to search for the 'English'. They whispered whether to take me or leave me in the car. In the end they finally left me in the car with the driver, a man with a very fat dark face with a big moustache, a very ruthless man. They went into the mosque because religious students or taliban lived there. The driver pushed the muzzle of his AK-47 into my chest and mockingly asked whether I thought anyone would rescue me now.

"All of this comes from Allah who is All Powerful and can do whatever He wants," I said.
He snickered and told me to make my entreaty to Allah for a rescue. He turned towards the old white-bearded man standing across from us in front of a shop. He asked whether the old man had any *naswar* (snuff). The old man said that he did, and at that moment I noticed that my bound hands didn't hurt as much as they had while we were travelling. I jiggled my hands and the turban knot came loose. I slowly took one of my hands out, keeping hold of the turban in the other hand. While the driver went to get tobacco from the old man, I opened the door of the vehicle and snuck out, but as soon as I was out I heard shots being fired by the driver.

I ran fast towards Deh Khwaja square while they were chasing me. At the square, a government-owned tank was parked and one of the soldiers noticed me. The solider stood in my way.
He seemed weaker than me, phsysically. I asked him a couple of times to let me go. He was not sure what to do. I pushed him out of my way and he fell on the ground. I started running again. I was by now on the Gumruk (Customs) Road and there were about ten guns firing from behind, but with the help of almighty Allah, I managed to get to the end of the road, unbelievable. I turned west on Mawlawi Obaidullah Jami Mosque alley. As this was the first alley on the road and since its end was closed off, many people had come out of their houses after hearing the shooting to see what was going on. I asked a few people to hide me, but they refused. I don't blame them, though, as they might have been frightened and did not want to get in trouble. A sister came out of the eastern door at the end of the alley, though, and bravely invited me into the house. Later on I found out that it was the house of a well-known businessman, Hajji Lalak Mama's accountant.
I was exhausted and my body ached all over from the beating. I was also extremely thirsty. I asked for water from the mujahed sister. She pointed to the water pot. I went to it and drank.

I was certain that the communists were still chasing me and that they would reach the house at any moment.
That didn't come to pass, however, since they were afraid of the guerrilla attacks that had become prevalent in all corners of the city. Following instructions from the sister, I climbed the walls on the eastern side, hung off the edge and let myself down. Allah was aiding me and I came down smoothly and unhurt on a pile of earth that had been brought to make mud. Otherwise I would have injured myself for sure since the wall was very high. I didn't feel well, though, so I went to Hajji Abdul Hai's house. He helped me and took me to Bala Karz area (outside the city) where my mujahedeen's houses were. From there I went on to Mullah Serajuddin's house where I stayed for two nights.

TRAVELLING TO PAKISTAN TO VISIT HOME AND GET MEDICAL TREATMENT

I had already intended to visit my family in Pakistan, but after the run in with the puppet soldiers I needed medical attention as well. Prior to the arrival of the car I had asked for, I went to Quetta through Spin Boldak on a motorcycle. I did not know where our house was, so I went to some friends and found our home address after receiving some treatment. My family had settled in Surkhab area of Pshin. When I saw my family, I became very sad; they were living in poor conditions. Also, being away from their country and homeland had added to their grief. I consoled them, though, and explained to them about the rewards and blisses of emigration. I stayed there for a short time, but the poor condition of my family and my love for jihad spurred me to get ready to return to our homeland soon.

THE RETURN OF THE MUJAHEDEEN TO ARGHANDAB

When all the aforementioned incidents had passed, when the Red Army had retreated from Arghandab towards the city of Kandahar, the mujahedeen returned to the area. They started clearing it, and before anything else they cleared Arghandab and the nearby areas from the defenders and the puppet government people that were left. There was a large military force based in the Khwaja Malik area. The mediators of the mujahedeen had negotiated with the heads of this military force and had convinced them to join the mujahedeen and surrender their entire force with its equipment to us. All of a sudden, some other government forces came and collected all the weapons from the Khwaja Malik force. Nobody knew how the government found out about our plan. It could have been the work of a government spy, or it could have been something else.

All of Arghandab was out of the government's control. By now the mujahedeen had become more powerful and were larger in number than ever before. Qari Azizullah's front in Pashmol, Esmat Muslim's front (who later joined the puppet government) in Dand, Hafiz Abdul Karim's front in Arghestan and Mullah Nasruddin's front in Spin Boldak were bases that were engaged in jihad against the Red invaders and the puppet government throughout Kandahar province. The number of jihadi parties had grown and some had split up to form new independent parties. The expenses of our front were being provided by *ushr* and *zakat*. The residents of Arghandab were giving us their share of *ushr* and *zakat*, but unlike other mujahedeen fronts we weren't receiving any support from the jihadi parties.

OUR FINANCIAL AND MILITARY CONDITION

There were many mujahedeen groups with us, so we had a lot of people. Most residents of Arghandab had left and the farms and orchards lay fallow. The few that were still being tended to were starting to face difficulties. The *ushr* and *zakat* that we had collected in the past was not enough to cover all of our expenses, and the jihadi parties did not provide any assistance to us. The mujahedeen ate only bread, and if they managed to find some *shlumbay* it would be a special meal for them. We spent most of our days inside our houses. In the mornings, helicopters flew overhead at very low altitudes searching for the mujahedeen in the orchards.

Our days and nights were full of problems. The helicopters of the Red invading forces gave us a very hard time. We would perform the morning prayers at dawn and then would move out to our safe areas, the locations of which were always changing. We were trying to find good weapons to use to defend ourselves. At some point we managed to get some heavy machine guns and other heavy weapons. At times we went into the city as well and would engage in jihad together with the other jihadi groups.

The mujahedeen were able to capture many weapons and other items as booty during the battles. It should be noted that, unfortunately, war booty was not equally divided according to the Islamic shari'a; the mujahedeen would mostly divide it up amongst themselves, in part because most of the mujahedeen were poor people.

Sometimes, we went to the orchards near Sanzari or Nazar Jan Bagh near Sarpoza to attack the supply convoys of the Red invaders that came from Turkmenistan. We burnt down tanks, military armoured vehicles, fuel tankers and other heavy machinery. These kinds of operations inflicted heavy and significant blows to the Red Army. In fact, it was thanks to operations like these that their war machine ground to a halt. Military convoys travelling to Arghandab, Pashmol and Mahalajat were also attacked. Sometimes these attacks lasted two or three days. The mujahedeen were able to resist strongly and severely damaged the convoys when they had enough ammunition and weapons. Sometimes, though, the Russians were able to put up a strong fight in return. The mujahedeen would travel long distances on foot and would move mostly during the night. That was the secret of their success. On the other hand, the Russians moved around in military vehicles and tanks, only rarely would they walk.

HOW THE MUJAHEDEEN GOT SUPPLIES

The Afghan mujahedeen put up a powerful resistance against the invading Russians. The clang of their swords and their zeal reached the world. A large part of the goal of the [Russian] invasion was to reach the warm water ports and occupy Pakistan and the region as a whole. America, the other superpower in the world, along with its allies were afraid of Russian expansionism so they decided to help the Afghan mujahedeen defeat the Red dragon in Afghanistan. Supplies of weapons was provided through Pakistan and over time better and more improved weapons started to come. Automatic machine guns and various types of heavy weapons were made available to the mujahedeen. They even provided Stinger missiles, which were very modern and sophisticated. Pakistan also managed to benefit from this exchange as the middle-man, and it equipped its own army with all these modern weapons. We would take the weapons given to us by our respective affiliate jihadi parties with cars to Afghanistan. Sometimes we were forced to use horses and mules inside Afghanistan. We were forever running into ambushes by the puppet government forces and the Russians, and would always get bombed by their war planes. We travelled at night with our car lights turned off to avoid detection by the Russian spy planes. Sometimes the mujahedeen convoys would be hit very hard in those attacks. Several mujahedeen would be martyred or wounded and the weapons would be destroyed inside the vehicles. In order to reduce these dangers, the mujahedeen started taking longer routes and would enter Afghanistan through mountains from Chaman. Sometimes they would go to Zabul or Anguri, then Tirin Kot and finally would arrive into Kandahar from there. The route was full of difficulties. After putting up with many casualties and damages, the mujahedeen were forced to ensure the safety of the highway. The mujahedeen used American Simorgh cars which had been tested in the region, and only later switching to Russian trucks, 8 cylinder motors the GAZ-66 Russian transport truck a Kamaz and Mercedez Benz-like truck for the transport of supplies.

THREATS AND PROBLEMS ON THE WAY WHILE TRANSPORTING WEAPONS: A STRANGE STORY

One time we were travelling to Kandahar with a Simorgh and a GAZ-66 truck. We also had another car that we had received from Mawlawi Khalis. Just as we were about to depart for Afghanistan, another mujahed commander — Talib Jan — joined us, increasing the number of those travelling to five. We entered Afghanistan from Quetta through Salison area where there was a river. There was a high likelihood that we would run into the puppet government along the way. There were rumours that a Herati commander called Ismael Khan had seized a large number of Russian weapons from an area called Buri near Shah Wali Kot and that Russians were patrolling all over. We reached the Kabul road via the Maltani route at Kharana Kuta. The road was blocked and many passengers and trucks were waiting. The dawn light arrived while we were still waiting. We went to the camp of a commander called Granai. There were many other vehicles there as well, a result of the crowded road.

Many people had gathered there. There were all sorts of people staying at the camp. Some of them were smoking hashish, others engaged in other vices. I couldn't stay there or put up with that situation. I tried to get out of that place by all means. We decided to move through the mountain and reach Daman via the paved road. It was a very dangerous route. Then we planned to turn towards Shahr-e Safa, which is very close to the main road. This is what we did in the end, but our car broke down on the road just before we turned off towards Shahr-e Safa. We found someone from the village who knew the way. He guided us past Shahr-e Safa until we reached Wakil.

At this point, we faced an even more imminent threat. We talked among ourselves and decided that I would travel ten minutes ahead of them driving the American Simorgh car. If I faced any problems, the second car would be safe. If it was all right, we would continue this way until we reached our destination. I travelled on ahead of them. After a short distance, the mujahedeen riding in the back of the truck with us knocked on the window to show me the flames could be seen behind us. It looked like something was happening to our fellow mujahedeen.

Unfortunately, we couldn't wait for them at that location, however when we reached the Rubat area of Daman where the road turns to Arghandab we stopped there and waited for our friends to arrive. The airport lights were bright and if we had turned on our vehicle lights the airport patrols would have noticed us. We spent some very tense minutes waiting there when finally our friends arrived. We learnt that the GAZ-66 truck had swayed from the road into a ditch and had rolled over, martyring a Talib mujahed who had newly joined the jihadi fronts. Another mujahed called Mawlana Fateh Mohammad Akhund was wounded. It was dawn by now, and even though the other mujahedeen cautioned against remaining where we had stopped, I stayed with some other mujahedeen and we went back to save the truck that had rolled over, full of weapons and ammunition. We continued on towards our destination. We agreed that one of our cars would take some mujahedeen and the weapons.
Daman was located between the city and the airport, so the Russians and the government forces would commute through

there several times per day. Tanks and military vehicles travelled to the airport. Military personnel and tanks would commute each day to draft people into military service.

RUNNING INTO RUSSIAN TANKS

We had sent one of the mujahedeen ahead of us to protect the overturned vehicle and we had taken up position in a nearby ruin. The mujahedeen hadn't eaten anything the previous night and we didn't have anything for the next day either. As soon as it got darker, we came out of our hideout and headed towards Daman road. We reached a village called Rubat.
When we reached Rubat village, we saw six tanks and two trucks carrying soldiers that were driving from the airport to Yungai village. The mujahedeen were worried that these tanks would come close to our overturned truck. We decided that two or three of our group should track the convoy to make sure our supplies were not discovered. We agreed to meet at Manja village to see whether the convoy route passed by our overturned truck.

Three of our Taliban mujahedeen got on their bicycles to track down the convoy. After two days and nights of hunger, we found something to eat. It was around nine that same night when the mujahedeen arrived in a car. We headed out to the area where we'd lost the truck, but a short distance from Manja we noticed something on the road. Moving a little further forward, we realised that it was the convoy we had seen earlier. There was only 20 or 30 metres distance between the two sets of vehicles so we couldn't just turn back. We kept going, and my car passed the first and second tanks that were parked to the side of the road. Suddenly, the third tank turned and blocked the road in front of us. We turned our car towards the desert and soon we reached the brook where our truck was located. It was a deep stream, so I shouted to Hassan — our driver, from Suzani area of Arghandab district — to accelerate. He told me that it wasn't working. He was still talking when a rocket landed next to him, taking his door off and wounding him. Martyr Mullah Abdul Haq Akhund was sitting next to me and the back of the car was packed full of mujahedeen. I got out. The Russians sent a flare into the air and the whole area became bright as day. The Mujahed next to me fell to the ground and his weapons fell away from him. I thought that it would be best to separate from the group and try to reach Zara Kariz area. Despite all the shooting, I quickly arrived at Tor Manda area where I felt a little safer from the Russian tanks. Since it was pitch black at this time of night, I had reached the area through a strange path. I hadn't been wearing shoes and there were so many thorn bushes in the desert. The thorns had torn up my feet. They were bleeding heavily and I only continue further with difficulty.

I got to the Tarnak river and after a short break I walked towards the house where I had had dinner earlier that night. The owner of the house became nervous when he heard the story, almost not letting me stay for the night. I didn't feel well and couldn't sleep. The weather was slightly cooler. I performed the morning prayer in the sitting position because my feet were preventing me from standing. I was extremely concerned about the rest of my mujahedeen, wondering what had happened to them. Who had been martyred and who had been wounded? What were the survivors going through? Where were they staying? I called on the owner of the house to check whether any mujahedeen had arrived overnight.
After about twenty minutes, the owner returned with one of my mujahedeen companions. He became very upset when he saw my condition, in the room without no heating in the cold weather. There wasn't even a blanket. He took me to the house where the other mujahedeen fighters had spent the night. They brought tea and bread, and we all ate.

Thank God that all the mujahedeen were safe and sound!
Soon enough, though, we started to think about our overturned truck with its load of weapons. We reached the main road and a passenger car stopped to pick up extra travellers. I reached the location of the last night's clash first, although there was nobody there by then. I spotted the AK-47 that had fallen to the ground the previous night. I asked the driver to stop, picked up the weapon and we reached the location of our truck soon after. I found that the truck had been pulled out of the ditch by the mujahedeen of Mullah Yar Mohammad, the man who would later become governor of Herat under the Taliban government. His fighters had taken the weapons to a safe location. We found

a 1620 truck to pull up our overturned vehicle. We towed it to a nearby garden and finally managed to start it. When we arrived at Shakar Ganj village (in Daman district), our truck broke down and we had to find another vehicle to pull the truck all the way to Arghandab. We finally deposited the broken vehicle in Arghandab and brought the weapons and ammunitions on a tractor to the mujahedeen front.

In short, transporting weapons and other equipment was extremely difficult for the mujahedeen. These trips would always be full of security problems. Many other interesting incidents happened along with the one I just mentioned.

It wasn't unusual for the mujahedeen to walk extremely long distances, even for twelve or thirteen hours. Journeys — such as going from Jelahor in Arghandab up to Siachoi in Panjwayi — were not easy, especially with all the Russian and puppet government forces there and because the mujahedeen didn't have any means of transportation.

There were other problems which were specific to these earlier phases of the jihad. These included walking long distances, air strikes and infantry pressure, surprise ambushes by the Russians, the lack of good weapons, poverty among the mujahedeen and public, and the relatively small number of mujahedeen in comparison with the enemy forces numbers.

The victory of the Afghan mujahedeen over the Red and wild occupying forces proved the verse of the Holy Qur'an correct: "A group with a smaller number of people will overpower the larger group." This was similar to Talut's remaining group of followers who must not have numbered more than 1300. The Afghan mujahedeen also shared many points with those who fought at the battle of Badr, the Prophet's first battle. Muslims have put up with many problems and difficulties.

The Afghan mujahed nation, even though it only had a few weapons and was fighting a global superpower that the entire world feared, achieved victory with the help of great God just as God helped the fighters in the battle of Badr [11].

HOW WE SEPARATED FROM MAWLAWI AKHTAR MOHAMMAD AGHA

Mawlawi Akhtar Mohammad Agha and the martyred Lala Malang sometimes had different ways of thinking, and some problems arose between them because of it. The mujahedeen had been through several serious disputes because of this clash of personalities. Many strong mujahedeen fighters quit our front on account of these problems and took up their jihad with other fronts and commanders.
For example, Mullah Naqibullah Akhund, Mullah Nuruddin Turabi and some other small groups had been fighting together with us, but they split. The martyred Lala Malang left our front several times, but I always went after him and brought him back; I didn't have any problems with anyone in our front. I respected all the mujahedeen and cared for them. I remained just as close to Mullah Akhtar Mohammad Akhund as I was to the martyred Lala Malang.

The difficulties between the two reached the point where Lala Malang would leave the front and Mawlawi Akhtar Mohammad Agha wouldn't even ask about him or pay any attention to this any more. One time when Lala Malang got upset and quit I informed Mawlawi Akhtar Mohammad Agha that I would go and bring him back. I left with a few other commanders from our front and went out to find him. We asked around at a few places and eventually found him in Arghestan at a front led by Commander Abdul Razaq. We asked him to return back to our front with us. He stuck to his decision and rejected our request at first, but after long discussions and a lot of reasoning with him, we were able to convince him. His one condition on coming back was that if he was mistreated again he would keave the front and that I would have to leave along with him.
We all accepted his condition and returned with the martyred Lala Malang to our front. Back at our base, the relations between Mawlawi Akhtar Mohammad Agha and Lala Malang continued to be poor. I cannot judge who was at fault. But I was then forced to fulfil my promise and follow Lala Malang after he left for the final time. Friends of ours suggested that I seek approval from Mawlawi Khalis' *Hizb-e Islami* to establish a new front. At that time, many of the religious clerics and Taliban stu-

dents were fighting under fronts affiliated with the *Harakat-e Enqelab-e Islami*, but these mujahedeen weren't really being paid much attention. The powerful fronts and mujahedeen like Commander Abdul Razaq, Mullah Hajji Mohammad Akhund, Mullah Shireen Akhund and some other groups had separated from *Harakat* and shifted over to Mawlawi Khalis' party. The mujahedeen seemed very happy with this, and they had more equipment as a result.

I left the area and by the time I arrived in Mesrabad it was night. I spent the night there and got some rest to be prepared for the long journey ahead. At dawn, when I intended to get going, suddenly twenty Russian helicopters appeared in the air and started heavily bombing us and firing rockets. The explosions got worse and worse and the mujahedeen were confused as to how the attack had started. The mujahedeen were running around desperately. Jet fighter planes arrived as well and started bombing the area. Early morning became dark night and still the explosions were heard all around us and the air was full of smoke and dust. Even the dogs were scared; they wouldn't stray from our company. As soon as the bombardment stopped, an unprecedented infantry force of Russians appeared and attacked from all four sides. They took up positions at both sides of Arghandab and advanced on Mesrabad. They also entered Taktu area. The forces that had entered Mesrabad and Taktu joined up together in Tughi area, close to the village where we were staying. We didn't have any special hideout there; the distance between the river and the mountain was 200 metres and the river was full of water making it impossible to cross.
Aside from Allah's mercy, there was apparently nothing else that could protect us. As always, with Allah's philosophy and guidance we unexpectedly found a large hole under some thorns and bushes where I, Sayyed Turak Agha and a newly convert to Islam from Hinduism hid ourselves. The Russians passed us by several times — even eating fruit from the orchards — without noticing us and once again Allah kept us safe.
Later in the afternoon, after the Russians left, we moved towards Taktu. On the way we noticed how the Russians had brutally martyred our fellow citizens in their homes. Many of our people were wounded. They had even killed the livestock and other animals. We returned to Mesrabad with great sadness

only to discover that twenty-two of our fellow Taliban mujahedeen had been killed and wounded. These were the bitterest of moments in our lives.

We cancelled the trip we had planned and took the martyred and wounded to the front. After the burial, a dispute arose over the transfer of the wounded mujahedeen. Some mujahedeen — with Mawlawi Agha at the head — had refused to allow us to use the car to transport our wounded mujahedeen. It was at that point that thirty-five other mujahedeen decided to leave that place with my group.

We rented a car from the town centre to transfer our wounded. Then we took the wounded mujahedeen from our and Mawlawi Akhtar Mohammad Agha's front to different places for treatment. We then decided to join up with Commander Abdul Razzaq's front until my return because there were many powerful and virtuous mujahedeen there. This front was well-known for its organisation and order. My companions and I believed that we could learn a lot from their virtue, order and loyalty. I left for Quetta accompanied by some of the Taliban mujahedeen. Some of their wounds were very deep and we wanted to give them proper treatment outside the country. In addition, I would work to make our new front official and also to obtain some weapons and ammunition.

In the end, our wounded mujahedeen managed to recover. Since our front was already quite well-known and because we knew many of the mujahedeen, we were able to quickly register with Mawlawi Khalis' party. To begin with, they gave us fifteen AK-47S and two RPGS. We took these weapons to our front and a short time later we got many weapons and ammunition, like the 8 mm mortar, heavy machine guns, medium range rockets, 72 mm artillery shells, ten AK-47S and many bullets.

OUR NEW TALIBAN FRONT

After officially establishing the front, the martyred Lala Malang and I sat with the other mujahedeen to consult with them on where we should open our front and where our jihad should be focused. I was happy to move away from Arghandab because I didn't want to be biased or to see to be showing off to my relatives and those who knew me. I believed that we should be devoting our lives to the path of the great God, his prophet, Islam and our homeland, and to keep far away from any kind of ethnic, linguistic or other enmity. In the end, we decided to open our front in the Pashmol area of Panjwayi district, and that's what we did. The people of Pashmol were very happy when we opened our front there. The people promised to help in any way we needed. They saw us very positively and treated us with respect and as their guests. Meanwhile, the mujahedeen tried their best to follow the path of Allah and his prophet.

ORDER AND VIRTUE OF THE MUJAHEDEEN IN OUR FRONT

We tried our best to keep some sort of order to our front and to our daily duties. We registered all the weapons that we distributed to the mujahedeen and tried to keep them in good condition. Everyone was responsible for his own weapon. We held training sessions and gave five cartridges to use at the range to practice their aim. If we weren't in a battle or training, none of us carried weapons around with us.

We organised a schedule of duties. Mujahedeen were required to pray their five prayers each day and anybody who violated this was assigned an additional two-hours of work or duties.

Nobody was allowed to fire a single shot without the express and prior permission of the commander or head of the front. Violations were subject to punishment. We consulted each other for any decision that needed to be made concerning the front, major or minor. We had a meeting to calculate our accounts at the end of each month and helped the families of the mujahedeen who were extremely poor if we could.

It was extremely important for us to be honest in our financial dealings. The use of drugs was completely banned for our front. Teenagers weren't allowed to be part of our front, either. No mujahed was able to travel into the city (or to stay there) without our prior permission. When the mujahedeen were sent to Quetta on jihad-related matters, each person was given 250 Kaldars to cover their transportation. We had rented a house in Quetta for mujahedeen and for our injured. Later on we also bought a car. We had some cars at our front as well which were used to transport mujahedeen from one location to another and to carry weapons and military equipment. We tried to provide everything that was necessary for the mujahedeen on our front to make their jobs easier. Later on we bought land near Nazar Jan Bagh and divided it up for mujahedeen to build houses. We provided construction materials and daily labourers. We bought cars and motorcycles for our leaders and for those with disabilities. We also sent some of them on Hajj.

OUR EFFECT ON THE PASHMOL AREA

When we first arrived in Pashmol, the other mujahedeen groups were extremely happy and our presence brought some unity among the groups. We conducted all our operations together. Those who had previously disagreed with each other no longer had any issues. Before we got there, the mujahedeen refused to distribute war booty equally among themselves, but when we arrived we informed them of Allah's and his prophet's words about war booty; this was enough to convince them to start distributing more equitably. There are many grape orchards in Pashmol. Some mujahedeen groups were collecting five Afghani for every grape vine, which was a lot of money. When we moved there with our front, someone suggested that instead of cash the grape orchard owners provide us with one-fifth of the crop instead. I could not accept this, though, and decided that our mujahedeen would rather endure poverty and difficult circumstances but not bother the public. We didn't want to busy ourselves with things peripheral to the jihad. I suggested that the other groups do the same thing and they agreed, ending agreements that were bothering the public. Of course there were still occasional disagreements and problems among the mujahedeen, but these slowly turned to brotherhood and love. The mujahedeen began to share expenses. There was no longer any objections if food was taken from one room to another, or for ammunition sharing, because we were sure that none of the items were going to waste.

THE INTENSITY AND RESULTS OF THE MUJAHEDEEN'S OPERATIONS

This was the time when the mujahedeen in Pashmol were united and when the mujahedeen in other parts also had good relations with each other. Accordingly, the mujahedeen operations against the Red Army and the infidel puppet government's convoys and bases intensified. The mujahedeen would ambush convoys at Sangisar and Pashmol every day, burning down tanks and military vehicles. There were even days when we would burn as many as a hundred tanks and military vehicles. The savage and infidel Russian forces faced unprecedented damages and were in big trouble.

In response, the Russians set up a security checkpoint in Abdul Qayyum Khan's castle and in Sangisar, manned by their special forces. Still, we continued our daily attacks and ambushes on the Red Army and puppet infidel government military convoys. We also placed mines on the roads leading to the newly-established checkpoints and attacked the checkpoint itself, adding to the difficulties the enemy was facing.

During this period, one night something funny happened. The martyred Lala Malang went to the Russian checkpoint on his own. When one of the Russian soldiers noticed him, the rest started firing at him. He managed to escape, however. The martyred Lala Malang was a very tough mujahed, and his bravery was well known. Once during an attack on the checkpoints, a new group of Russian soldiers arrived to support their forces. Lala Malang went ahead on his own, got up close to this group and threw a hand grenade at them. They were all killed. He took a Cuban AK-47 from one of the soldiers. He kept it with him at all times and left it for me when he was captured.

THE CAPTURE AND IMPRISONMENT OF LALA MALANG

When I had to bring weapons for our mujahedeen for a second time, I bought an American Simorgh car (for which I would have to pay at a later date) because of our poor financial state. When I returned to the front, the martyred Lala Malang told me that he wanted to go to Pakistan. This was just three months after we had established our front.

I wasn't there when he left, and when I returned I found out that he had gone, so I went to look for him. I joined up with him at Mullah Dad Akhund Ghondai area where we had several friends. We spent the night at Hajji Nek Mohammad's house. We went to the mosque at dawn for the *fajr* prayer. We came out after the prayer but Lala Malang stayed inside. We returned to

Hajji Nek Mohammad's house. When the sun had risen, news spread that the infidel government had conducted a search in the area. I was with another mujahed friend of mine — Hajji Turak Agha — and we ran to our motorcycles outside. Just as we were about to drive off, soldiers shouted at us to stop. We left the motorcycles and ran into the orchard, and from there, ran off to another area called Kaghatak. It was there that we heard the heartbreaking news that the martyred Lala Malang had been captured by the infidel government soldiers.

We became very upset and returned through the orchards for the most part, thus avoiding the main roads. When we got back, we saw Lala Malang arrested. We didn't have any good weapons with us, just pistols. We fired at the soldiers and they returned fire. There weren't many soldiers there and they feared we were part of a larger mujahedeen group come to release Lala Malang. They left the area in a rush, taking him and three of Hajji Nek Mohammad's sons with them.

The mujahedeen of all of Kandahar province were struck by grief and the people were also upset by his arrest. Hajji Nek Mohammad's sons ended up being released in exchange for a Russian soldier, but Lala Malang remained in custody.

Lala Malang's father, Mawlawi Sadozai Agha, had mediated to exchange the three sons for a Russian soldier that had been captured by Sayyaf's mujahedeen. But Lala Malang remained in the custody of infidels and the responsibilities of the front rested completely on my shoulders. I had, after all, been his assistant in the past.

We sent the late Mawlawi Serajuddin to Kabul to meet with Lala Malang. Three successive courts of the infidel government had issued a death sentence for Lala Malang, but the case had been taken all the way up to the presidential level, that of Dr Najib. Some steadfast friends had made this possible — like the late Hajji Abdul Ghafur who was himself a powerful mujahed and always helped out. The president personally waived the death penalty for Lala Malang, so instead he was confined to prison for an unknown amount of time.

OUR FRONT'S ACTIVITIES DURING LALA MALANG'S IMPRISONMENT

We intensified our operations and continued our jihad as usual while Lala Malang was in custody. We fought in different areas at night and during the day. The Russian invading forces conducted operations in Pashmol at least once a week. Their infiltration operations by infantry units also increased. Although they had set up checkpoints on the main paved road, we had more or less blocked them, so the invading Russians' convoys had to use a point in the desert that was out of reach of the mujahedeen weapons.

When we realised this, we would go there at night and plant land mines to blow up the Russian tanks and vehicles. I will give an example. One time, a Russian military group with heavy and light weapons came to Pashmol. They spread out quite quickly, but the mujahedeen were on alert and the battle began. We quickly killed their main shooters and afterwards the mujahedeen came out of the orchards and killed the rest of the Russian group. The Russians didn't even have time to respond. All their weapons and equipment were taken as war booty. The weapons were AK-47s, PK guns, RPGs and bullets, all of which were later distributed among the mujahedeen.

THE WITHDRAWAL OF THE INVADING SAVAGE RUSSIANS' CHECKPOINTS

The savage Russians tried very hard to clear the road for their convoys and they didn't spare us any kind of horror or barbarism. They shed the blood of many innocents, destroyed many houses and villages and even killed animals and burnt orchards. Still, though, they were unable to secure the road and whenever they used the desert route they would still be hit by land mines, as would the tanks and military vehicles travelling to the checkpoints. The mujahedeen also carried out mortar attacks on the security check post during the day, even getting as close as twenty metres. The security checkpoints were not only unable to secure the roads, but also not their own safety. Many of their soldiers were killed and suffered extensive material damage. At some point, the mujahedeen received the

107 rockets which were able to reach the Russian convoys passing through the desert and their checkpoints as well from far away. The increased financial and human costs forced the Russians to abandon those checkpoints and retreat five kilometres into the Zheray desert. We set up joint checkpoints and placed forty or fifty mujahedeen in each of them. These mujahedeen were tasked with bringing the Russian checkpoints under fire. The mujahedeen's trenches and hideouts were spread all over the area. The mujahedeen conducted night patrols to protect the mujahedeen bases and the residents from Russian attacks.

THE MARTYRDOM OF A WELL-KNOWN TALIB MUJAHID, MULLAH NAJIBULLAH

Once, Mawlawi Najmuddin came to our front to visit the mujahedeen. He was Mawlawi Khalis' representative in Quetta. He sent me a message asking me to come to Chenarto area of Shah Wali Kot, a relatively safe location. I went together with Mullah Hajji Mohammad Akhund. While we were away, a Russian guerrilla group martyred two very strong Talibs of ours and threw their bodies into a well. The Russians had taken their PK guns and escaped. When we returned from Chenarto, we planned an intensive attack on the Russian guerrilla groups and agreed that we would fight to the death.

It was the holy month of Ramadan and some mujahedeen came to inform us of the surprising appearance of the Russians. It was a sign of unity among the mujahedeen that when I issued a request, hundreds gathered together. We went hastily to Faiz Mohammad's place, from there to Wazir area and then we spread our mujahedeen out all over. There were well-known mujahedeen at this battle, like Mullah Burjan Akhund and Mullah Mohammad Akhund.

I directed the mujahedeen to wait while I went (together with two strong mujahedeen) into the Wazir area and started searching. We didn't find any sign of a Russian presence, but when we reached Hajji Abdul Rahim Qala I noticed that there were PK guns on the rooftops. I indicated to my fellow mujahedeen to turn back and hide. We left quickly.

All the mujahedeen shared the opinion that we should start the attack in the afternoon because it was Ramadan and we didn't want to become very tired and allow the enemy to benefit from this. We decided that one group lead by Mullah Burjan would encircle them and fire at the Russians and that the second group would attack the Russians in the afternoon. We started the assault as planned and the mujahedeen fought bravely, forcing the Russians to retreat from the area after some brief resistance.

APPEARANCE OF THE RUSSIAN FORCE AT NIGHT

In all the battles I witnessed, no mujahed was ever taken hostage by the Russians. Real mujahedeen would either win their fight or fight until they reached the high goal of martyrdom. The savage Russians didn't spare any tricks. Sometimes they would come as a large military force to search and clear the area, and sometimes they would send small military groups to conduct guerrilla operations. Other times they would surprise us with night raids.

In one attack by the invading Russians, several mujahedeen were martyred and wounded. After that happened, we decided to go to Khakrez district and ask Wahab Khan for a 75 mm mortar. The mujahedeen wanted to destroy the Russian checkpoints using the mortar. When we reached Sanzheray we looked for a safe place, because we preferred to travel at night and to rest during the day. This helped us because we could avoid facing the Russian and puppet government forces directly. We always came out onto the main road at night. We could see when a Russian convoy was coming from the city; we could see the dust rising in the air and their lights at night.

I was together with another strong mujahed, the martyred Rahmatullah, a Waziri man who commanded a small group of mujahedeen. I told him that this convoy was heading towards Pashmol and that they were hoping to destroy mujahedeen bases in a surprise night raid. He thought that it was a Russian convoy on its way to Herat. At any rate, we thought it best to continue on our way and wait until the next morning to see what happened. As we had agreed earlier, the mujahedeen moved into the bases and living rooms and we all got together to plan for the upcoming battle and operations. After a long discussion, we agreed that the mujahedeen should go to the trenches and set up high positions so that they were in place before the Russian attack. We tasked some mujahedeen with the supply of weapons, and some special individuals were assigned to patrol at night. During this patrol they had to carefully watch the Russians' movements.

At dawn, I went with some mujahedeen to the trenches and found everybody performing their duties as planned. By sunrise, the Russian convoy came from the desert. The Russians were coming straight from the main checkpoint — there was an area in the desert known as 'loy posta' or main/big checkpoint where there was a large Russian military base. When they reached the road, they stopped and set up their artillery and mortars. Afterwards, they fired on the mujahedeen trenches and bombed us from the air with their jet planes. Infantry followed the bombardment, firing on the trenches and making life extremely difficult for them. When the fire started to ease a little, I wanted to go to a location where some mujahedeen had been heavily hit by the Russians. When I tried to run there, a tank fired at me. The shell landed (and exploded) extremely close by and half of my body was buried in earth. Some mujahedeen quickly pulled me out. We had barely reached the trench that had been hit when it was hit again by the Russians. Russian tanks were moving in alongside the infantry. I put out a message to all the mujahedeen to hold their fire. The Russians were moving forward very boldly because they thought they had killed all of those on the front line. When they were just thirty metres away from our trench, I ordered the mujahedeen to open fire. The invading Russians came under fire from all four directions, something they never imagined. All the savage soldiers were killed quickly and six of their tanks were burned. The Russians faced an amazing resistance and were confused by the heavy casualties. The remaining soldiers and tanks retreated in haste under the cover of air strikes.
In short, this battle continued for a second day since they entered Pashmol after their day of heavy casualties. There, too, they faced a strong resistance and the brave mujahedeen shielded their chests from the savage Russian bullets. Several mujahedeen were martyred, including Mullah Abdul Hadi Akhund and Mullah Salim Akhund. The battle was drawn out and the savage Russians didn't spare any force or horror. More

than five thousand bombs, thousands of mortars, artillery and rocket strikes were used. Many tanks, armoured vehicles and other military vehicles were destroyed and hundreds of soldiers were killed, but with the help of almighty Allah they weren't able to defeat the mujahedeen.

THE STRENGTH OF THE MUJAHEDEEN'S FIGHTING MORALE

The morale of the mujahedeen was extremely high as they were used to many different types of battles, tactics and tricks. We had also received some good weapons, even allowing us to fight face-to-face against the Russians. I recall that once a Russian guerrilla group came to Pashmol to conduct operations against the mujahedeen. The mujahedeen faced them in the Wazir area where there were many orchards. They fought against the Russians and encircled them completely. They weren't even able to evacuate their wounded soldiers. There was only a wall standing between us and the Russians; there was a water brook nearby. The Russians had pulled their wounded over there so as to attend to their injuries, but the mujahedeen fired on them from four or five metres away. When we reached the spot, we found the brains of the injured Russians spattered and splattered all over the place. All of the Russian group had been killed in the battle.

A BIG FORCE IN PASHMOL AND ITS DEFEAT

A few days and nights later, the Russians prepared a large force to avenge the previous defeats and damages that we had inflicted. Around a thousand different tanks and military vehicles were part of this convoy. They chose their battlefield: a location close to the river and the desert. They hoped to easily enter Pashmol from here.

The mujahedeen, on the other hand, insisted on preventing the Russians from entering Arghandab because once they managed that, the likelihood of defeating us in the battle was considerably higher.

The Russians had learnt their lesson from previous engagements and so took up positions in the orchards close to their trenches. The mujahedeen were equally numbered in terms of infantry, but the invading Russians were backed by jet planes, helicopters and tanks. They were able to damage the mujahedeen bases very easily. The battle lasted three days and the savage Russians managed to capture the mujahedeen's trenches after heavy bombardment and artillery fire at the end of the third day. I was very sad that night. A mujahed called Tor Agha asked for some ammunition from me to head out with a group to recapture the trench. Even though it sounded impossible, I gave him the ammunition.

At around dawn we heard the sudden fire of heavy and light weapons. Moments later Tor Agha came to me to let me know that he had captured the trench. He requested some extra mujahedeen to allow him to hold it. I went with a few others. We saw the bodies of Russian soldiers cut into pieces. Some were without their heads, and some were cut into half and in pieces. We put up a strong fight after that, and even made some gains. After a heavy battle, almighty Allah granted the mujahedeen victory once more. Even with all their force, they weren't able to enter the area.

Several mujahedeen were martyred and wounded. My assistant, Rahmatullah Jan, was martyred in this battle too. I later selected Mullah Obaidullah Akhund to replace him; he later became the Minister of Defence during the Taliban's government. I should note that the BM12 rockets and mountain mortar helped the mujahedeen a lot in this battle against the Russians, because the mujahedeen didn't have weapons like this in the past. All of the examples I have been mentioning are just illustrations of broader trends. We had many similar battles and fights. They were daily matters and it is not possible to mention them all or this book would become too long.

EXCHANGING LALA MALANG

The martyred Lala Malang was spending tough days and nights in Pul-e Charkhi prison. Earlier I mentioned how he had been given a death sentence by the infidel government courts and how that sentence was commuted to life imprisonment after the mediation of some mujahed friends.

In the meantime, Mullah Mohammad Ismael Akhund had captured a Russian soldier during a battle. Mullah Mohammad Ismael Akhund was a powerful mujahed commander who was first with us at Mawlawi Akhtar Mohammad Agha's front but who later opened his own front. We always had good relations with him. After he took the Russian soldier, he started to make efforts to exchange him for Lala Malang. He had contacted the Russians and the infidel government about this issue and the Russians had agreed. I was informed about this by Zabit Abdul Jalil, Mullah Mohammad Ismael Akhund's brother-in-law. He told me that they had been working on exchanging the martyred Lala Malang and that they were hopeful that it would work out.

At the time, I was very busy with the jihad. The mujahedeen were very well equipped and our political affiliate party was providing abundant weapons and other military equipment. In addition, there were lots of training programmes on fighting tactics. In short, the jihad was moving forward very strongly and the mujahedeen were becoming powerful in all aspects. Our front had drawn the attention of the party's higher officials because we had many great and strong mujahedeen fighting for us. Our jihadi groups were mostly located in areas like Charbagh, Pashmol and Sabzkar where the war was a constant presence. We also had two groups lead by Mullah Tor Akhund and Mullah Mohammad Lal Akhund who were well-known in the whole of Kandahar province for planting mines. For these reasons, the equipment and weaponry available for our front increased, making our front one of the best-equipped and most advanced in terms of our access to the newest weapons. The party officials always took the people of our front for training, sending them back with many light and heavy weapons. The jihadi trench was warm and strong while the invading enemy looked tired, frustrated, defeated and desperate.
The business of the exchange for the martyred Lala Malang was proceeding slowly. All of our friends did their best and went through tough situations that made them very tired. I did not rely on these efforts, however, and I was even told that Mullah Mohammad Ismael Akhund had changed his mind. At this time, the puppet government brought Lala Malang to Kandahar airport to exchange him. I received a cassette on which we could hear his voice to confirm that it was really him; he was humbly asking Mullah Mohammad Ismael Akhund to carry out the exchange to get him out of the horrible conditions and that

he had been brought to Kandahar airport. He added that doing so would be a very big favour that he would never forget. I became sad listening to this cassette and the mujahedeen cried a lot after hearing his voice. We assured the mediator from our end and told him that they would know our final decision in two days.

MY LAST EFFORTS FOR THE EXCHANGE

I went from Pashmol to Nakhunay in order to bring up the issue with the great mujahed and cleric, Abdullah Zakr and Commander Abdul Raziq. They promised any help they could provide and accompanied me to Baladeh area to talk to Mullah Ismael Akhund. Baladeh was Mullah Ismael Akhund's focal point. When we arrived there, Mullah Ismael Akhund's mujahedeen said that he had gone to Arghandab. Since we didn't have much time, I convinced Commander Abdul Raziq that we should follow him to Arghandab as well. We set off to Arghandab. Those days, the Russian supply convoys would come from Turkmenistan every other day. We were travelling on the day of the convoy. Whenever the convoy was passing, the Russian security forces would put new security measures in place and block the roads for the public. It was especially difficult — even impossible — for the mujahedeen to travel at those times. We were forced to spend the day in Mirbazaar until the convoys had finally passed in the evenings and when local patrols had decreased. We passed Herat road and got onto Arghandab road. We hoped to find Mullah Ismael Akhund that very night. We found his car in the cemetery but he was not there. I knew that he was there but that he was hiding; I suspected his tribesmen had made him exchange the Russian soldier for Mullah Sabir (a judge from his tribe) who was being held by the Russians. We went to Khwaja Malik's place that night and talked the issue over with Zabit Abdul Jalil. He confirmed my suspicions and said that Mullah Ismael Akhund was hiding from us.

We went to Zalakhan area after crossing the main paved road and then went back to Baladeh from there. We waited for Mullah Ismael Akhund to return to his focus point in Baladeh. Around ten o'clock the next day we heard from the Russians that they were waiting for our decision. Mullah Ismael Akhund had not yet arrived, so once again we went out looking for him. On our way, we saw him returning with Mullah Naqibullah Akhund. At the focus point, Mr Zakiri brought up the issue with Mullah Ismael Akhund with Commander Abdul Raziq, Mullah Naqibullah Akhund and other mujahedeen present. He psychologically prepared Mullah Ismael Akhund to accept the exchange. This was despite the fact that Mullah Ismael Akhund had initially said that Lala Malang was a powerful mujahed and that he could help the mujahedeen a lot, while Mullah Sabir was just an old man. He had changed his mind on account of pressure from his tribe and Mullah Naqibullah had supported the decision.

THE LAST PHASE OF THE EXCHANGE OF A RUSSIAN SOLDIER CALLED ABDULLAH

After long discussions, he consented to the exchange. The Russian soldier who was being held by Mullah Ismael Akhund was of medium height, twenty-two years old and from a family of White Russians in Moscow. He had converted to Islam and taken the name Abdullah. He was a military tank specialist with the mujahedeen then. He had started religious studies, too, at Mullah Ismael Akhund's front. We informed the mediator that we were ready for the exchange. We agreed to meet at nine o'clock the next morning in the Sarpoza area.

Next morning, I went towards the end of Mirbazaar (close to Sarpoza) together with Commander Abdul Raziq, Mullah Naqibullah Akhund and around a hundred other mujahedeen. We took up positions there, and the Russians also brought their forces and took up positions with their tanks. We sent a message that both sides needed to observe a ceasefire during the exchange and that we would have five elders sit with them from our side as a guarantee. We agreed on the location and said that they should bring Lala Malang on a motorcycle and that we would bring the Russian there in a car. Both sides fully observed the ceasefire. There were even some KhAD members who travelled to the mujahedeen areas that day knowing that they would not be attacked. I sat in the car with the Russian soldier and moved towards the exchange venue. Upon my arrival, they arrived with

Lala Malang. We took him from them and returned to Zalakhan along with the rest of the mujahedeen. We spent the night there — the first night following his release — and then moved towards Pashmol. All the mujahedeen were very happy with his return, but unfortunately Lala Malang's brother, Mohammad Yaqub, was martyred a short time after that.

THE EXPANSION OF THE WAR AGAINST THE SAVAGE NON-BELIEVERS

Our front received 107 types of rockets and at that time we were the only front with access to that many rockets. Our mujahedeen launched about one hundred rockets on the airport from Daman Landai village. We then followed up in the second volley with twice as many rockets. The mujahedeen of our front were the first to attack the airport with Sakar-20 rockets even though they had to pass through two tight security belts with thm. We set up a joint checkpoint led by Mullah Burjan Akhund and the mujahedeen in Pashmol. There were many mujahedeen at this front. With their help, we passed the Sakar-20 rockets through the infidel government forces' security checkposts.

One of my brothers, Ali Mohammad Agha, was martyred there. He was a really strong mujahed who always had his gun by his side. He performed the holy jihad against the savage invading Russians and was finally martyred by the explosion from a shell fired by a Russian tank. On that day I went to Mahalajat to fire some rockets. Mullah Mohammad Akhund and the rest of the mujahedeen had already brought the weapons and ammunition. Mullah Mohammad Akhund was a military commander during the Taliban time and was martyred in Dilaram. I tasked the mujahedeen with taking care of the funeral affairs of Ali Mohammad Agha and to bury him in Pashmol. Mullah Mohammad Akhund and the rest of my friends and elders insisted that I go along to the funeral. They added that they would put the enemy under harsh weapon fire.

I went to Pashmol for my brother's funeral. Mullah Mohammad Akhund and the mujahedeen conducted very effective attacks on the airport. This way our mujahedeen were also the first to launch DC and 12-M mortars against the airport. Such attacks were very effective and were causing a lot of damage (both financial and human) for the savage enemy. We tried to make these attacks constant and not let up. On account of our attacks and the heavy damages they had suffered, the Russians relocated most of their jet planes to Shindand airport.

THE MARTYRDOM OF LALA MALANG

A large military convoy of the invading Russians moved towards Arghandab. That Russian force stayed for about a month in Arghandab. Lala Malang decided to fight. I told him that I would also go, but he said that I shouldn't because I had participated in so many battles while he was in prison. Lala Malang set out on his way along with some other mujahedeen for the purpose of jihad. The savage Russian forces had gone to Charbagh area where our mujahedeen base was located. I received some reports from the mujahedeen that a large Russian force was in the Sanzari area and that they were pounding the mujahedeen with heavy weaponry from there. The mujahedeen agreed that if a group were able to place fire on this Russian force from the rear, they would be distracted and the mujahedeen in Arghandab would be able to go about their business.

We went with a group of mujahedeen to set up a 12 mm mortar in the Ashgu area and then to put the new Russian force under fire from there in order to give the Arghandab mujahedeen some relief. We finished our work but before we started to fire, a messenger came and delivered the news of Lala Malang's martyrdom to us. I quickly went to Mirbazaar area, which is close to Charbagh. We first made sure the mujahedeen had left the area in order to release them from the enemy's blockage. Some of our friends were stuck there. That night we didn't go to Charbagh but instead went to Pashmol and started firing heavy weapons against the base in Sanzheray. That way we put pressure on the base and eased the conditions for the mujahedeen in Arghandab.

At this point something amazing happened. I would like to mention it briefly. The mujahedeen put a 12 mm mortar in a tractor and moved towards Ashghuri. When the tractor reached the Wazir area and got on the main road they found they were facing a Russian convoy. One of the Russian tanks left the road and drove straight towards the mujahedeen at a very high speed. It seems the Russian soldiers inside the tank were drunk or that they had lost their way. The mujahedeen did not lose their morale, though, and opened fire on the tank as soon as it got close enough to the tractor. The tank was destroyed and all the occupants were killed. They took all their bodies except one of them, from whom the mujahedeen took a Kalashnikov rifle as booty. We buried the Russian soldier under a wall.

The next day, some of the Russian forces in Arghandab came to an area called Abdul Hamid Khan and pressured the locals to show them where the Russian soldier was buried. They took the body of their dead soldier with them and they left the area. The next day we went close to Charbagh and entered the area when it became dark. Lala Malang and other famous martyrslike our friend Abdul Qadeer Sahebzada (from Sahebzada village of Daman district and the son of Mohammad Shoaib Sahebzada) were lying in the mosque. It was not possible for us to take their bodies that day. We had a rule in our front to try our best to bury the mujahedeen martyrs were they were martyred and not take them anywhere else. In any case, this area was close to our ancestral home, Jelahor. For these reasons we buried the martyrs there and moved back to Pashmol that same night.

The people of Arghandab had suffered a lot at the hands of the Russian forces and they asked us to help them with some weapons and mujahedeen. We agreed to send them five hundred well-equipped mujahedeen along with some good mine planters like the late Mullah Lal Mohammad Akhund. This big group of mujahedeen was led by Mullah Burjan Akhund and Hajji Hayatullah Wardak. A heavy battle broke out and the Russians once again displayed their full power. They used all their force ranging from infantry to artillery, tanks and other heavy weapons supported by air strikes. The Kandahar Corps commander, Juma Asak, and the Russians had decided to win this battle with the cost being the destruction of the whole of Arghandab and the use of all their power. This huge force was defeated after the firm resistance of the mujahedeen though, and at the end with the help of great God. In addition to the seizure of many weapons and military equipment as war booty, the mujahedeen captured many soldiers as well. The Kandahar Corps information unit chief was among those captured.

OUR CHARBAGH MUJAHEDEEN'S OPERATIONS

There was a large and strong group of our mujahedeen based in Charbagh area. This group would conduct operations in the city and in surrounding areas. Most of the time they would attack the Russian army convoys. There were popular mujahedeen such as my old friend, martyr Talib Jan, who was an expert in hitting tanks. He burned many Russian tanks in his time. So many tanks were burned, in fact, that in the end the Russians used these burned tanks as shields against mujahedeen operations. Nevertheless, they didn't help them much in preventing the mujahedeen operations and they continued apace.

The Russians had set up a defensive security checkpoint on top of Baba Ghazi and Murghano hills. Our mujahedeen attacked those checkpoints often, hitting the tanks travelling there or killing two or three of the Russian soldiers. In short, the Russians had a tough time in Arghandab and they could spend a single moment in peace. There was a stream near Nazar Jan orchard where the Russians would swim and the mujahedeen would plant mines there. They would explode while the Russians were swimming resulting in the amputation of their legs.

THE STRANGE ACTIVITIES OF SOME OF THE MUJAHEDEEN

Mullah Abdul Nafi Akhund was a hero mujahed from Takhtapul district of Kandahar province. He was a virtuous, responsible and highly motivated person. Thanks to his good behaviour, all the mujahedeen respected him and all admitted to his bravery. One of Mullah Abdul Nafi Akhund's brothers was also a mujahed with us and he was martyred. His parents had passed away and he did not have a family.

At one point, the mujahedeen were attacking Kandahar prison and the battle had been prolonged. A supply tank travelled to the prison at a very high speed and the mujahedeen were not able to hit the tank although they tried several times. Mullah Abdul Nafi Akhund came to me in Pashmol and asked for my permission, saying that the armoured tank could be hit. I did not want to give him permission for such a risky attack because he did not have any family members or relatives and the mujahedeen cared for him so much. Early in the morning, I asked the mujahedeen where Mullah Abdul Nafi Akhund was.

They said that he couldn't wait and had gone to hit the tank. He had taken an 82 mm rocket from the Charbagh area with him and had gone to our joint checkpoint near the prison to watch for the tank when it would come in the evening. At the time he knew the tank would approach, he went out onto the main road and fired the rocket at the tank from a very close distance. The tank fell into a nearby stream. After the mujahedeen victory, there was a tank lying in the stream and it could have been the tank that took supplies to the Russian checkpoint located on Baba Ghazi hill, west of Nazar Jan orchard and that was hit by Mullah Abdul Nafi. Mullah Abdul Nafi Akhund was wounded several times during the jihad, so there were scars all over his body.

During the jihad, the Russians once sent a big force to Pashmol. Throughout the battle, I went to check on the mujahedeen in all the different trenches. Mullah Abdul Nafi Akhund accompanied me, but he left me at some point and when I checked to see where he was I saw that he had been injured by a mortar shell detonation. I went back to our base to see how he was. I saw that he was sitting up and when I asked him how he felt and where he had been hurt. He smiled and joking asked me to walk behind him and ask the same question.
When I walked round the back, I noticed that his vest was covered in blood and that his back was wounded very badly. There were cuts all over his body, shrapnel was stuck in his back, but he was very humble and patient and didn't complain about his wounds at all.

On a separate occasion when I was in Chaman, I heard news of some injured mujahedeen arriving. At the same time, the vehicle arrived with the injured. I quickly went to the vehicle and saw Mullah Abdul Nafi among the wounded mujahedeen. His leg had been cut in a mine explosion. I couldn't bear this and started crying as this was the eight or ninth time he had been wounded during the jihad. He smiled and told me not to cry.
The wounded mujahedeen were treated in the Red Cross hospital. When I went there, the doctors told me that my friend Abdul Nafi was a very tough man. Most of the time he would ask the doctors not to give him anaesthesia when they carried out their surgical operations. The doctors would operate without

anaesthesia but he would not show any signs of being in pain during the operation. Mullah Abdul Nafi Akhund's jihadi activities are so numerous that we can't mention them all here, but I wanted to give some remembrance to them.

MARTYR MULLAH BURJAN

Mullah Aminullah Akhund, also known as Mullah Burjan Akhund, was from Taloqan village of Panjwayi, Kandahar. He was a mujahed on Mullah Hajji Mohammad's front, but in reality he performed jihad on many different fronts. He would often lead joint groups in Pashmol, Sangisar and Nelgham. He never grew tired of the battles of the jihad and his faith and stability in the path of jihad was very strong. He saw all mujahedeen as being equal and did not discriminate between Talibs and ordinary mujahedeen. He did not like wasting time back at the base or hanging around there. We had very good relations and he respected me greatly.

There was a joint group in Mahalajat that Mullah Burjan had brought together as a sign of unity. He led that group for years and nobody ever grew upset with him during this long period. He was always very frank and respectful. He would also consult me in all matters. During the Taliban's government, he was sad about how I wasn't involved and he would often tell me that my impartial stance made him want to quit the movement. He came to Kandahar in a helicopter several times, trying to get me to go with him to Charasyab. but I did not accept for two reasons that weren't convincing for him. My brother, the martyr Ali Mohammad, was at a joint checkpoint together with him and was later martyred. Mullah Burjan himself was finally martyred on the Jalalabad-Kabul road in 1996.

MULLAH MOHAMMAD AKHUND

Mullah Mohammad Akhund was from Manari village, Arghandab district, Kandahar. He was a mujahed with me from when he was very young. He received some religious lessons while he was on our front. I taught him *Sarf Bahayee* and some other books; I was his teacher. Mullah Mohammad Akhund was very smart in his jihadi skills. He was a good leader and mostly lead small mujahedeen groups. His comprehension was good and he was a military commander during the Taliban time. He was the second most senior Taliban military commander post-1994, but he was martyred in Delaram.

TALL MULLAH AHMAD AKHUND

Mullah Ahmad Akhund was from Azan Nawa village, Kajaki district, Helmand. He fought jihad on the same front as us. He was a brave and zealous mujahed, never scared while in battle. He was well-known for his bravery among all mujahedeen. Sometimes when he was travelling to the battle, the rest of the mujahedeen would joke with him and ask whether he was in a hurry to get them into trouble.

The Panjab big stream passes by the Sarpoza area and is usually dry during the winter. The Herat highway passes near the same area; in fact, the road is crossing over the stream. Mullah Ahmad Akhund — together with four or five other mujahedeen — would hide himself under the bridge in the stream and would attack the Red Army security tanks as they passed overhead early in the morning. They would block the passage of the convoys and spent the whole day fighting with them. The Russians would bombard and strike the mujahedeen ambushes with their artillery. After heavy financial and human loss, the Russians would leave the area in the evening.
Mullah Ahmad Akhund was a very humble and kind person. When someone joked with him, he would smile and look down out of modesty. He was very virtuous and God-fearing and would listen and obey whatever directed to do. He never violated orders.

MULLAH MOHAMMAD LAL AKHUND

Mullah Mohammad Lal Akhund was from Rikwa village, Panjwayi district, Kandahar. During the jihad he was well-known for planting mines on the routes of the enemy. His sharpness and sense of where was the best place to plant the mines led to the destruction of many tanks. He planted mines all the way from Sarpoza to Sangisar for the Russian convoys. He was so talented in planting mines that he invented some new ways of doing this. His mines never failed to detonate.

Mullah Mohammad Lal Akhund tried his best to avoid spending the *Bait ul-Mal*, the shared money used by the mujahedeen. He was virtuous and keen to perform jihad, but had no interest in becoming famous at all. He was injured three times during the jihad and finally reached his real wish for martyrdom.

COUNTRY-WIDE COUNCIL

There was a council made up of jihadi commanders from all over the country. Its purpose was to coordinate mujahedeen operations around the country and to lower mujahedeen casualties (and to make them stronger). The jihadi parties didn't show much interest in this council, however.

I was present at the founding of the council. At first there were twenty-five commanders representing different areas that had gathered and met first at Mawlawi Jalaluddin Haqqani's house in Miranshah. From there we went to the base at Zhawara and, after talking there, agreed to invite jihadi commanders from all over the country to join the council.

Many more people showed up for the second meeting, including Mawlawi Jalaluddin Haqqani, Commander Abdul Haq, Mohammad Anwar Jegdalak, Tulwak Arsala Rahmani, myself (representing Kandahar), Mullah Mohammad Rabbani from Wardak, Mullah Shireen, Qazi Mohammad Amin as well as Commander Musa.

The third meeting of the country-wide council was even bigger still. I went to represent the mujahedeen of Kandahar. Mullah Mohammad Rabbani, known as Hajji Mawin during the Taliban time, was the deputy head of Commander Abdul Raziq's front. Hajji Mawin had very good relationship with me. When I went on the Hajj, the Rais-e Baghran, Mullah Abdul Wahid, was with me in addition to Hajji Mawin. Hajji Mawin was a very humble and virtuous person. He was a God-fearing man, always keeping himself from saying bad things about others. He worshipped a lot and loved Medina and Mecca. We fought many battles together. I will mention only the battle in Qalat at this point. The operation lasted three months and we were both wounded in an assault during that battle. We were taken to the same hospital. We accompanied each other to the country-wide council meetings. In fact, we went there together twice.

The important point that the meetings sought to accomplish was to see coordinated operations. Each of the participants would talk in turn and discuss the problems and offer possible solutions. For the fourth meeting of the council, we were busy with our military operations. One of the new participants at that meeting was Commander Ahmad Shah Massoud. Hajji Mawin and I weren't able to attend that meeting.

For the fifth meeting we were able to attend and it was held later in Zhawara in Mawlawi Jalaluddin Haqqani's house. This was the last meeting of the council before the mujahedeen took over Kabul and collapsed the puppet government shortly after that. The Russians launched Scud missiles against the base and the surrounding area while we were having our meeting.

WHO ENCOURAGED THE ESTABLISHMENT OF THE COUNTRY-WIDE COUNCIL AND WHO BENEFITED FROM IT

We found out later on that the country-wide council was supported by the Pakistani government and that its finances were paid by Pakistan following the wishes of America. The United States, along with other western countries, wanted to prevent the Russians from moving forward in Afghanistan. At the same time, they didn't want the mujahedeen to be a significant force after the Russians were defeated. So they established and supported this council to reduce the power and authority of the jihadi parties.

After the council was established, the commanders with close ties to Pakistan received a lot of support and this brought about disunity and power struggles among the parties. More money was taken by the commanders based in Peshawar. They were getting several times what was being sent to the other parties elsewhere in the country. Some of those commanders received hundreds of millions in cash. People like Mawlawi Shireen Akhund and I, though, and other great commanders did not get anything. There was no justice in the distribution of funds and everybody was trying to secure as much funds as possible for himself. There was no care for their fellow mujahedeen.

Many commanders used to attend the council meetings just to get money or other benefits paying lip service to jihad. Our mujahedeen were very keen to perform jihad and tried their best to coordinate and organise operations but unfortunately personal interests and desires were preferable to jihad and to the country's interests and wishes. This was the main reason why the council did not last long and why its plans were never implemented.

DEFEAT OF THE RED ARMY AND OUR CONTINUATION OF OPERATIONS AGAINST THE REMAINING PUPPETS

When the Russians finally admitted their embarrassing defeat after ten years of war with such high financial and human costs, they were forced to leave Afghanistan. This unforgettable and golden day was recorded in gold script in the history books. This was a great victory and moment of happiness for the mujahedeen and increased their confidence and morale. The Afghan people were happy that their problems, sacrifices, pains, casualties and emigration and many more problems had resulted in this great victory.

If we look back a few years in our history we can see that after the monarchy system we had Sardar Mohammad Da'ud Khan who went to Iran and Pakistan to try to improve relations. He also made trips to Saudi Arabia, Egypt, Kuwait, India and France to discuss development and strategic issues, even signing some agreements. These efforts were beneficial for the country and the region, however our powerful neighbour was suspicious of these efforts. The Russians were against this policy of the Afghan government and they did not want to see any western influence in the region because it was thought to be against Russian interests. In order for the Russians to demonstrate their power to Iran and the other western-influenced country of South Asia, Pakistan, they started spreading Communist ideas among some ill-minded Afghans. Then a Communist party was established and it quickly took power in a coup. The Russians noticed that this wasn't effective enough so they decided to invade directly on December 27, 1979. Tens of thousands of their military forces entered Afghanistan, occupying major Afghan cities and the capital, Kabul.

The Soviet Union was a world superpower at that time and had the largest territory consisting of twenty-five countries. The international community, especially the United States and its allies, were afraid of the Soviets' increasing power. And here were the Soviets shamelessly attacking a small neighbouring country whose government was already on their side. They imposed untold atrocities on a poor nation. After a long war of ten years, using all of its powerful and modern weapons and bombs, it was defeated by this empty-handed nation.

In my opinion, there were two reasons for this victory of the Afghan oppressed nation. On the one hand, the Afghan nation did not spare any sacrifice or problems or hardship. On the other hand, the struggle was based on religious and shari'a principles. It was like the war between Talut and Jalut during the time of Shamoyel (PBUH) when Talut's followers did not want to fight and only three hundred of them stayed with Talut. Still, Talut put his faith in God and believed in victory. Almighty Allah says in the holy Qur'an:
"Tell those who believe they are going to meet Allah that sometimes a small group will be enabled to overcome a larger group."
Another example are the Badr fighters who fought against the non-believers in the path of God and victory of Islam and finally succeeded with the help of God. In the same way, Afghans engaged in jihad were very faithful to their religion, homeland and honour when the Russians invaded Afghanistan.
Most Afghans were unaware of politics and of the false and deceitful behaviours related to it. They did not associate with any particular group and nobody put their personal goals or benefits above those of others. They all followed one religion and hated un-Islamic thoughts and actions. Since the people in Afghanistan and other Islamic countries opposed the awkward Communist ideas and actions — and though the invasion of Afghanistan was the beginning of a larger invasion of Iran, Pakistan, Kashmir, Bangladesh and against Indian Muslims — they all reacted firmly and rose up as a serious obstacle standing in the way of the Russian occupying and invading forces.
Most of our neighbours — especially Pakistan and their tribal people — were on the same page and that is why they supported the Afghan nation. Other large and powerful countries like America and Britain helped the Afghan nation through the jihadi parties out of fear of the Soviets and for their own interests. The Afghan nation received these funds out of ulterior motives and spent them on this war in which America sought to take revenge for the Vietnam War. This was a good oppor-

tunity for them to infiltrate and influence South Asia as well. That was why they increased their support for the jihadi parties. This was an opportunity for the newly established deceptive Pakistani government and its intelligence agency. The Pakistani government only gave part of the funds that came from the US and the west to the mujahedeen. They hid the bigger portion of it and spent it on its own military.

The west believed that Afghanistan was the best place where they could have influence in the region, because it would be easy to enter when opportunity presented itself. An example of this is their current invasion and presence in Afghanistan. America and the westerners wanted to increase their influence in the region so they brought the mujahedeen and the remnants of the puppet government to fight against each other after the Russian defeat. They created hatred among the people over religious sectarian, ethnic and many other issues, paving the ground for their coming here and spreading war and instability. America and its allies spread a lot of propaganda against Islam, jihad and Muslims through various outlets. They also painted a dark and awful picture of Islam and Muslims to other international countries by reminding them of those wars. They killed the good Muslims and mujahedeen through their own conflicts, or defamed them in other ways. This is how they made their expansion of power possible in the region and showed themselves as competent powers for other countries.

AFTER THE RUSSIAN WITHDRAWAL

After the Russians left Afghanistan, the mujahedeen remained a large and organised force. The defeat of such a big power had really improved the mujahedeen morale. The enemy was left by itself, helpless. By that time, the savage Russian bombardments, the use of heavy weapons and the death of hundreds of oppressed innocent people (including women and children) had been stopped.

Before that, the mujahedeen were on a dual track: in a both offensive and defensive status. Nevertheless, they were not as powerful. By this time they were only on the offensive. We began our infiltration operations very quickly in Kandahar.

At first we cleared the checkpoints around Sanzheray very easily.

Then we decided to capture the main Silo and launched two days of operations. The mujahedeen captured areas near the city as well. We blocked the supply route from Kukranu. Two days later, the puppet government soldiers fled from the Silo area and the mujahedeen took it. The mujahedeen captured many light and heavy weapons, wheat and other food items as war booty. The mujahedeen moved forward and attacked a checkpoint in the Baba Ghazi area which was located on a hill top. We continued on towards Murghanu Ghondai and Jandarm checkpoint.

The mujahedeen approached Kandahar's main prison but it was unfortunate that the mujahedeen were not coordinated and organised at that time. If we had attacked Kandahar City from all sides, we could have captured it but that is not what happened. Only the mujahedeen from Pashmol managed to capture all the checkpoints leading up to the prison.

The soldiers in the prison had taken up positions in fortified trenches. All the other parts of the prison, meanwhile, had been fortified with stone, making the mortar strikes less effective. After that, the mujahedeen intensified their encirclement and set up a seventy-man checkpoint at the location. Mullah Mohammad Akhund, later a Taliban military commander, was the head of that checkpoint. His assistant was Mullah Abdul Razaq, later the Taliban minister of commerce and then later still arrested by the Americans and taken to Guantánamo prison. The soldiers of the puppet government put up strong resistance and martyred and wounded several of the mujahedeen. The mujahedeen dug three big holes from the northern part of the prison through the houses at the Abasabad area. We came thirty metres closer to the prison and wanted to block their supply route completely.

An armoured tank that used to bring supplies to the prison was finally hit by Mullah Abdul Nafi after many failed efforts by other mujahedeen. I mentioned that story before. At this point, a group of mujahedeen managed to dig a hole from behind the prison into the building itself. I entered in that hole and was able to take eight or nine inmates out of the prison. The battle continued. A large mujahedeen base was set up on Mullah Saheb Dad Akhund Ghondai or Hill. When Mullah Mohammad Akhund was not present, we put Mullah Dadullah Akhund in charge, who, despite his young age, had excellent leadership skills. Mullah Dadullah Akhund was one of the very first Taliban commanders later on. During the jihad he fought with Mawlawi Akhtar Mohammad Agha's front and performed the jihad with great bravery. He was a daring person.

Our mujahedeen were busy with jihad in many different locations and were preparing to conduct operations in Arghandab against the district governor's office. It was later captured after a heavy battle. From there, Panjwayi district was captured as well. The mujahedeen placed DC and 122 mm mortars in Suzkar base and put Kandahar airport under fire from there. Those strikes turned out to be very effective because the Communist puppets were forced to relocate their planes and helicopters from Kandahar airfield to Shindand and to evacuate Kandahar airport.

MAHALAJAT CIRCLE MILITARY OPERATIONS

Hoping to encircle Mahalajat, the infidels surrounded Mat Qala area in the old city and around Kandahar airport to block mujahedeen movements from Pashmol, Arghandab and other areas. They also wanted to prevent the Mahalajat mujahedeen's operations in the city. The puppets wanted to divide the mujahedeen up and spread problems among them so as to separate the various groups. At the same time, they wanted to keep the Mahalajat mujahedeen surrounded. Despite these efforts, the mujahedeen continued their battles and came in from other areas. We had a joint checkpoint there that was led by Mullah Burjan. That checkpoint was considered the right arm of the mujahedeen and a powerful base. The mujahedeen in that checkpoint were changing quickly. For the first time, 122 mm mortars were fired on the airport from the checkpoint and I conducted that operation myself. One night I wanted to go there, but my brother, Sayyed Ali Mohammad Agha, was martyred that night. Still, I did not want to return for his funeral on account of the eagerness and enthusiasm I had for jihad. But the mujahedeen, friends and Mullah Burjan Akhund advised me to go to the funeral and the prayer ceremonies following the burial. So I left Mullah Mohammad Akhund in my place and I went to the funeral.

MAHALAJAT CIRCLE OPERATIONS

In short, the mujahedeen were strong and always travelled between their bases. There was an infidel checkpoint in the Zheghateru Band mountain area. A plane would take supplies and drop them in an open area and then the soldiers from that checkpoint would collect them and bring them back to their checkpoint. It was impossible to supply them in any other way. Our mujahedeen would ambush that area and take all the supplies for ourselves.

At this time, most mujahedeen from Kandahar gathered together to carry out a big assault on the infidels' encirclement. We prepared ourselves and the battle broke out. Most parts of the siege lines were broken by the mujahedeen and many tanks and military vehicles were burnt in addition to inflicting heavy casualties during this battle. As a result of the operations, Mahalajat road was reopened and the mujahedeen resumed their movements between bases.

The infidel government's military forces decided to recapture the lost checkpoints, however. The mujahedeen also prepared themselves and attacked the circle. Some of the mujahedeen were injured — like Mullah Mushr Akhund, who was a great mujahed and was martyred during the Taliban time — but they captured two more checkpoints even though the mujahedeen operations were not as intense as previously.

The puppets gradually retreated towards the city after a long battle that saw us break the entire circle. The puppet government military wanted to set up another ring of security around the city after they were pushed back. But by that time, the mujahedeen had expanded their operations to all the places near to the city. When Najib's infidel government was left on its own and its Red Lord had fled they wanted to make two deals with the mujahedeen. Firstly they wanted to buy off those who loved money, and secondly they wanted to eliminate the real, honest and saintly mujahedeen.

At that time, most operations in Kandahar were being carried out by the Taliban mujahedeen or by those who were really fighting in the path of God. Noor ul-Haq Ulumi and Sardar Akram were working in Kandahar on behalf of the infidel government and they managed to buy off many mujahedeen. The mujahedeen went through many problems and found it tough to find places to conduct operations. One day the Watan Front (Khalqi Communists) arrested five of our mujahedeen and destroyed the DC mortar that was placed in front of our base. Mawlawi Saifuddin, who was our friend, was shot dead by Lala Jan. Unfortunately, people like this have always created problems in our community. They tried their best to place obstacles in front of the real mujahedeen. As part of this plan, they placed landmines on the paths of the mujahedeen. Mujahedeen tanks and mortars were destroyed in Arghandab. Some people were arrested trying to destroy our tanks in Panjwayi; they were executed in public following a trial.

Things like this took place all over the country, however the real mujahedeen continued on their path and finally toppled the infidel government. The mujahedeen gained victory and they established a government in Afghanistan.

AIRPORT MILITARY OPERATIONS

After the Mahalajat encirclement was broken, there was only one checkpoint left at Mard Qala mountain near the airport. The mujahedeen first attacked the checkpoint and then the battle expanded to the flat areas nearby as well. We took an armoured tank as war booty from Mard Qala checkpoint.

By then, Kandahar airport was the only important military base still in control of the puppet government All the mujahedeen groups and the political parties in Kandahar focused their attention on the airport. The mujahedeen set up a storage area at Nakhunay in Panjwayi district because the mujahedeen had so many weapons and equipment by that point. They needed a location near the front line to store it all.

The mujahedeen conducted operations against the defensive lines for a while and then we changed our plan and decided on more extensive operations against the airport.

Some were happy and others were not about this decision. Those who weren't happy about this operation were receiving some personal benefits. At any rate, the mujahedeen eventually managed to start the operations. We made Khushab, Qazi Kareez of Mullah Abdullah village and the surrounding small villages our centres and began our operations.

The mujahedeen were able to advance forward to the southern and southwestern parts of the airport initially, and they surrounded the airport quite quickly. The mujahedeen got very close to the base and even were able to target its centre with machine guns and mortars.

Mullah Mohammad Akhund was leading this battle. Kandahar airport is located in a strategically important area in the south of the country and it was of vital importance to the Communist puppet government. It was obvious that the loss of this airport would mean the collapse of Kandahar province, so they really did not want to lose it. They threw everything they had at us. The battle continued for around five months, in fact. The jihadi parties wanted to end the operations against the airport and return the mujahedeen to other operations in the city and surrounding area, but our mujahedeen did not want to carry out attacks in the city where there was a high likelihood of causing civilian casualties. We tried to conduct operations during the night on specific targets, but civilians would get hurt most times.

At that time, the representatives of most jihadi parties had come to Kandahar. Mawlawi Najmuddin, commander of Khalis' party and his Quetta office head, Abdullah Khan Wardak, were there, as was Zabit Karim, the commander of Harakat-e Enqelab-e Islami and others. They also tried to get us to refocus on other parts of the province rather than just Kandahar airport. Based on our previous experience, however, we didn't want to carry out operations in residential areas where the likelihood of harming civilians would have been higher. Since those representatives were our guests, we respectfully convinced them and told them that smaller operations would be conducted in the city, but not extensive ones.

Many mujahedeen were martyred and wounded in the airport battle; the puppet government forces also suffered heavy casualties. Heroic mujahedeen like Mullah Abdul Nafi Akhund were among our martyrs. Mullah Sakhi Akhund was paralysed due to severe injuries, but still he has become a great cleric thanks to the jihad and its blessing. Hundreds of Talibs listen to his instructions. May Allah further increase his blessings and allow him to succeed on the path of serving Islam.

THE DESTRUCTION OF PLANES

Our mujahedeen hit three planes from Najib's puppet government forces and they crashed. We hit one near Sultan Mohammad Khan Kareez in Daman. That came down in an emergency landing. We hit two others in the Shahr-e Safa area, and even arrested the pilots of one of them. The pilots were later exchanged for mujahedeen being held in government custody. The mujahedeen of other fronts were present in these attacks alongside our forces. All the planes that crashed were supply planes on their way to Zabul. The government used to bring in their supplies in military cargo planes.

THE TALIBAN'S OPERATIONS IN ZABUL; OFFICIALS' COUNCILS

International donations were transferred to the mujahedeen by Pakistan. Pakistan would keep much of the funds for itself. Inside Afghanistan a system was set up by the mujahedeen. Depending on the size of the operations, local councils were set up in each province. Each council designated someone as their head. Six local councils were set up in Kandahar. I was selected as the head of our area council. Others included: Mawlawi Sayyed Akhtar Mohammad Agha, our former head of the front; his friend Mullah Dadullah Akhund, a well-known figure during the Taliban's rule; Mullah Shireen Akhund and his friend Mawlawi Abdul Hanan; Mullah Mohammad Sadiq Akhund and his friends Mullah Abdul Salam Zaeef, Taliban ambassador to Pakistan, and Mullah Obaidullah Akhund, the Taliban minister of defence; and Mullah Mohammad Omar Akhund, who was later chosen to be the Amir ul-Mu'mineen, and his friends Mullah Baradar Akhund and Hajji Hayatullah. I would bring supplies for all of these people from Quetta and we were all together for our operations.

I was away from Kandahar when some mujahedeen moved towards Tirin Kot to carry out some operations there. They neglected to inform the mujahedeen from our front, however. When I returned, most of the mujahedeen were upset that they had not been invited to come along. I calmed them down and told them that we would soon get ready for our own operations. I was head of the Council and we were in a relatively good finan-

cial condition. I gathered the Council together and we met that same night; we agreed on operations in Zabul.
We decided to first send someone to talk to the mujahedeen there and inform them of our intention in order to pave the way for our arrival. Mullah Mohammad Sadiq Akhund was selected for this duty. He was a strong mujahed and had a powerful Taliban front. After the fall of the Taliban, he was arrested by the Americans and sent to Guantánamo. He was released later on after spending some time there. Mullah Mohammad Sadiq Akhund went to Zabul and returned after his meetings with the mujahedeen there. He told us that the mujahedeen needed help and that they had agreed to our plan to come to Zabul. We invited some mujahedeen from various bases and left for the neighbouring province. We first took up positions in the Garm Aab area. I should also mention that Mawlawi Khalis' party provided us with 400,000 Kaldars to support this move, which was helpful in taking care of our expenses.

Mullah Shireen Akhund, Mullah Obaidullah Akhund, Mullah Baradar Akhund, Mullah Mohammad Sadiq Akhund, Hajji Hayatullah Wardak, Mawlawi Abdul Hanan, Mullah Mohammad Akhund and around fifty other powerful mujahedeen accompanied us for this journey.
The battle started just when we reached Garm Aaab and we were able to capture the checkpoint there. We had some armoured tanks during this battle, so it was very interesting. The mujahedeen moved forward and three days later we attacked and captured a checkpoint known as Jadid, located south of the Kandahar-Zabul road. After placing a security force there, we returned to Kandahar. Soon after, though, the puppets suddenly attacked and recaptured their checkpoint and some other small checkpoints as well.

We heard news in Kandahar that a large military force was headed to Zabul. Jabbar Khan's brutality was legendary and he was preparing to strike the mujahedeen with his massive force. We held an emergency meeting to prepare for the battle. Mujahedeen from Zabul were present at the meeting as well.
We wanted to send our own mujahedeen to face the troops mid-way, allowing the other group to stay in Zabul to fight. The Zabul mujahedeen didn't like this idea, though, and refused

our request to attack the incoming force. After we insisted, Mullah Abdul Salam Rocketi and Mullah Abdul Karim — both of whom had fronts in Zabul — came with us. We sent around five hundred mujahedeen led by the martyred Mullah Mohammad and the martyred Mullah Yar Mohammad to confront the force. We didn't hear back from them for some time. The force neared Zabul. Mullah Rabbani Akhund, Mullah Abdul Salam Rocketi and Mullah Abdul Karim went to confront the incoming troops together with some other mujahedeen. We faced them near Kharan Kutaa and clashed in a heavy battle. The puppet government forces intensified their efforts using tanks and artillery, and the battle got heavier from one moment to another. The mujahedeen were running out of ammunition. In short, their force overpowered us and scattered the mujahedeen.
I was left alone with a friend called Abdullah — who was later Mullah Mohammad Omar's driver and martyred in his home during an American raid. We climbed a hill near the battlefield. We were very tired and as soon as we reached the top of the hill the enemy noticed us and put us under mortar fire. We ran away, pursued by the onslaught of heavy weapons fire. I asked Abdullah for water and he gave me his water container. We reached the bottom of the hill and were so exhausted that I could barely even see any more. Mullah Mohammad Akhund and Mullah Abdul Hanan were coming towards us. Abdullah wanted to fire a PK at them, but I told him to wait until they were closer. When they got up close, we recognised that they were our friends.

From there, we decided to go to a place called Anka, a mountainous valley south of the main road, in order to find somewhere for the mujahedeen to hide. Several mujahedeen were martyred and wounded in that battle. Two Arab mujahedeen were also among the martyrs. After the burials of the martyrs, we return to Zabul and met up. We agreed that we couldn't defeat the force without first splitting the force in half. Three hundred mujahedeen from our joint front — including the members of Mullah Mohammad Rabbani, Mullah Abdul Salam Rocketi and Mullah Abdul Karim's front — immediately prepared to head out.

OUR SUCCESSFUL OPERATIONS

We headed towards Shahr-e Safa, deciding to first attack some checkpoints on the main road so as to distract the main force in Zabul and to deprive the enemy of those posts. This way the force would split into two parts on its own. The mujahedeen fought and took over the checkpoints one after another. In other words, we completed the first phase of our operations successfully. As we approached Shahr-e Safa, we picked Sayyedanul village as a place for the mujahedeen to gather.

The puppet government had two types of installations in Zabul on two sides of the road. With the help of great God we were able to get information on the military strengths of both sides. After engaging them in a heavy battle, we were able to defeat both. The infidel government forces bore a heavy material and human loss. An armoured tank was among the booty that the mujahedeen took.

SEIZING PLANES

At the end of the battle, we contacted the groups led by Mullah Mohammad Akhund and Mullah Yar Mohammad Akhund on the radio. As soon as they learned of our victory their morale was raised and they were inspired to attack the infidel forces in Manja area of Daman district the next day. The puppet regime forces used their full power and brought additional troops, weapons and ammunition in helicopters there. The military helicopters were seized by the mujahedeen as soon as they landed and the mujahedeen attacked. The battle lasted longer and the mujahedeen moved forward.

Finally, the mujahedeen defeated the puppet government forces and seized many light and heavy weapons. They took a 40-cannon mortar, a Sakar 30, DC mortars, armoured tanks, vehicles and many other items as war booty. We took one of the helicopters to Arghestan with the pilots, but the other was destroyed during the battle.

The mujahedeen continued their filtration operations in the area and removed it from the control of the puppet government. The road was cut and a large part of the big force that had advanced on Zabul faced a very serious condition. It was impossible for it to retreat, and they could only move on to-

wards Zabul. The remaining part of the force unwillingly went ahead; they didn't want to leave the main road, though, so they decided to go from the bottom of the mountain in Jeldak just to get to Zabul alive. The mujahedeen found out about these plans in advance and decided to lay a trap for them.
We got in our 4 × 4 pick-up trucks. The morale of the mujahedeen was so high that they would have gone head-to-head with an armoured tank in those pick-up trucks.
We seized another armoured tank and two military vehicles from the puppets near Hindwano Paliz area of Jeldak. They escaped and the force was stuck near a mountain called Carola. The mujahedeen launched their assault at night and went forward. They found out that the tanks and the military vehicles were there but the troops had fled to the Kuchis' area.
We estimated that some 175 soldiers had escaped, all of whom bore weapons. The mujahedeen went after them and captured the soldiers with their weapons. The mujahedeen didn't leave the tanks either and went after them.

They were able to stop the tanks at Zariku area and to seize all their weapons. In addition, the mujahedeen took many other weapons and equipment as war booty during this battle. Many armoured tanks and military vehicles were burned.
The force commander, Jabbar Khan, managed to escape through Daman road. The mujahedeen inflicted great financial and human damages to the enemy and also arrested many troops. Although I believed that the captives ought to have been released in the circumstances, they were given to the court to be tried. The court was overseen by the great cleric, Rohullah Akhund, and Mawlawi Abdul Salam.
As the council demanded, all the mujahedeen moved back to the province to plan for another battle. The mujahedeen were divided into four groups and attacked from four separate directions. There were many Arab fighters as part of our group and we sent them to participate as well. They were very keen for jihad but we could not let all of them take part in the operations. The Arab mujahedeen asked me to allow all of them to fight in the battle. I told one of them to remain at the base to take care of the base and equipment and I allowed the rest of them to participate. The one who ended up staying behind was called Abu Talha.

Early in the morning when we wanted to leave, Abu Talha came to me and said that although he had been selected to protect the base and its materials he would prefer to protect us and go with us as a bodyguard. I agreed, and although he fought very bravely on the battlefield it was his destiny to be martyred that day. One of the soldiers had entered a hideout and I wanted to go after him but Abu Talha went ahead of me saying that he was my bodyguard. He was shot and martyred upon entering the hideout.

Another Arab mujahed, Abu Tayyeb, was martyred in that battle as well. Of course, it wasn't just me and my mujahedeen who were participating in this battle, but also Mawlawi Shireen Akhund and his mujahedeen — including Mullah Abdul Hanan and Mullah Abdul Haq — and Mullah Mohammad Sadiq and his mujahedeen — including Mullah Abdul Salam Zaeef, Mullah Obaidullah — and Mullah Mohammad Omar Akhund and his mujahedeen like Mullah Baradar Akhund, Hajji Hayatullah and other mujahedeen. Hamidullah Tokhi was also present. We asked him to guide us on the way but he said that he didn't know the full way very well. He was afraid that he would take the mujahedeen through a path that was a minefield. We asked Commander Jabbar, but he did not have any information either. We were discussing this issue when the attack on the rest of the checkpoints started. Our meeting was happening at a small mosque. When I came out, the mujahedeen were complaining about the extreme cold weather. The mujahedeen's operations had started, though, so I took them with me and left the meeting. When we approached Rahdar checkpoint we split the mujahedeen up into groups. Mullah Obaidullah Akhund led one, Mullah Habibullah Hanafi led the second and I led the third myself. We engaged the checkpoint from four sides and managed to gain entry within fifteen minutes. Mujahedeen from the council arrived as well and we seized many weapons and military items.

Only one of our mujahedeen was injured in a mine explosion and Abu Talha was martyred. After the battle we let the leaders go and I remained with the mujahedeen. When we woke up early in the morning we talked in detail about the mujahedeen operations. We were all on the same page that the checkpoint was in direct view of the government forces and that it would be hard for us to keep it. We decided to leave it. All the mujahedeen groups contributed a lot in that battle and we achieved something great together. The cold winter weather, snow and rain had blocked the mujahedeen supply routes so we found it better to return to Kandahar. The light and heavy weapons, tanks, military vehicles and other military equipment seized as war booty were distributed among the mujahedeen according to the shari'a.

DOSTUM, HIS GELIMJAM MILITIA AND THE TALIBAN MUJAHEDEEN'S FIGHT AGAINST THEM

A month later, the puppet government sent the Gelimjam militia led by a commander called Abdul Rashid Dostum to supply Zabul. The mujahedeen met together at the council level and reached Wanduz area in cars. Mujahedeen from some other areas had also reached this point. We had our meeting and were planning operations.

We agreed to first attack the checkpoint located in the Shir Ali area. I believed that we should attack a weaker point in order to infiltrate their areas (and also to ensure that we would succeed by weakening the enemy's morale and to raise our own morale) some other mujahedeen believed that we should attack the strong checkpoint first. I was put in charge of the operation together with Hajji Mawin Mullah Rabbani.

There was a hill in the area, and the puppet government forces were on the top of the hill. We divided the mujahedeen into three groups. One led by Mullah Rabbani was assigned to the east of the hill, another led by me was assigned to the south of the hill and the third was to approach from the west of the hill. All three groups attacked the first trench as soon as we climbed the hill. I thought that the trench was captured so I went on ahead, but some of the enemy's men were still there and they threw a hand grenade at me. I was hit in my leg and was injured very badly. With God's mercy I did not end up in their hands like Hajji Hayatullah, a commander affiliated with the Ittehad-e Islami party and together with us on the council. Mullah Mohammad Anwar, the head of the Baghran mujahedeen, and Atta Jan took me away from the battlefield as soon as I was injured. They carried me on their backs for about two hours.

Mullah Rabbani Akhund was also wounded in this battle. Mullah Atiqullah Jan was one of the bravest mujaheds of our front and he was martyred soon after I was wounded.
The battle ended for two reasons. Firstly, Mullah Rabbani Akhund and I were both injured and we were the heads of two of the battle groups. Secondly, there was so much rain coming down and the rivers were full of water. It made it difficult for the mujahedeen to carry their supplies. The puppet government was able to continue bringing their supplies for their people in Zabul that winter.
I stayed in the hospital for nineteen days and recovered fully by the mercy of Allah.

THE VICTORY OF AFGHANISTAN'S MUJAHEDEEN

It was the holy month of Ramadan when I went to Mecca on Umra together with Mullah Mohammad Hassan, the martyred Mullah Ahmadullah Akhund and one of our great clerics the martyr Mawlawi Serajuddin Akhund. During our stay there we got word of mujahedeen victories so we rushed back to Afghanistan. When we arrived in Pakistan some provinces had already fallen to the mujahedeen. We went back to Afghanistan and Kandahar without delay.

After talking to the mujahedeen and getting information, I found that the mujahedeen forces were divided into two parts. Unfortunately it was very obvious during those days. One group was the Taliban and their fellows who were the real mujahedeen and who did not have any relations or contacts with the puppet government and its militias; the second group, however, had relations with the puppet government. They had signed an agreement with the puppet infidel government to prevent the real mujahedeen from entering the city. Most of the real mujahedeen were not aware of any of it when we reached Kandahar, however the other group had taken up positions around the city. We quickly got in touch with them and asked them what their plans were. They had divided their commanders into two groups as instructed by General Akram. One of their groups was supposed to keep the mujahedeen busy in the areas near the city so they would not focus on the city. This group was based near the Silo area. The second group was supposed to

gather its people together and take control of the city.
We went and had a meeting with them, but this plan did not sound right to us. In the second meeting, we insisted that an emergency council should be established in order to take control over the city, to keep order, to make sure that the provincial affairs weren't neglected and to make sure that everyone was assigned a particular job. They didn't want to discuss these things, though. We also asked the people in the meeting about how they had assigned to take control of the city, because those people were not attending the meetings, but we never got a straight answer.

We continued to insist on the establishment of the emergency council. Anyway, they finally contacted General Akram and he surrendered the city to them. They entered the city and everybody tried to take control of a part. One took over the army division; one took over the police headquarters, the governor's office, the intelligence division, and so on. Each group that had entered into some kind of compromise or bargain got to keep the institution that they had been in contact with. All the miseries and discord that followed derived from this point.
The mujahedeen were split up into various groups. We all got together and decided to go to the airport, but we were prevented from going there, even to the point that people wanted to fight us over it. We didn't want to fight, though. A few of our mujahedeen had a dispute with a soldier, but I didn't know about it. Anyway, I didn't want the dispute to get worse.

In short, the internal disputes and disagreements among the mujahedeen was part of the Communist' plan. The love and caring for each other that had been part of the mujahedeen way was gone. Our [Taliban] mujahedeen did not want to get involved in the internal clashes, so we decided to return to our former bases. We were not willing to work together with the people who collaborated with the communists, because the communists had spared no efforts to destroy this country and to kill this oppressed nation. Our principles also did not allow us to fight against our mujahedeen brothers.

OUR COUNCIL

After these incidents, we set up a council outside the city and chose an area called Dafi Hawa Ghondai (Air Defence Hill) near the airport as our base. There were many mujahedeen in this council, and Commander Abdul Raziq was elected head. One of the objectives of the council was to keep the mujahedeen powerful as in the past and to negotiate with the officials in Kandahar about ways to reach this goal and to establish a transparent administration in Kandahar. Unfortunately, some people only care about themselves and were ready to violate the rights of ten people just to make sure that they get what they want. When these kinds of people are in power, they don't let anybody else share the responsibility, particularly if they might end up questioning their selfishness or get a share of the benefits. We tried several times and even contacted the central government to establish an inclusive administration.

Along with many jihadi commanders, we came to Kabul when Hazrat Sibghatullah Mujaddidi was in power. We met him in the presidential palace. During the meeting we pointed out the gaps and shortcomings of his government to him. We also expressed our dissatisfaction over the collaboration with Dostum, who was a criminal. We added that doing so did not conform with either the country's or the jihad's benefit. Our suggestions and comments went unheeded. During the meeting his comments mostly focused on how he could stay longer in power and he asked us how we might help him do this. He repeated these things several time during the meeting. The government had arranged for our stay at Ariana Hotel, where the mujahedeen broke many alcohol bottles. This really upset Hazrat's brother. Our delegation met with several of the jihadi leaders, like Mawlawi Mohammad Yunis Khalis, Pir Sayyed Mohammad Gailani, Burhanuddin Rabbani and Ustad Sayyaf. We also had a meeting with Hekmatyar outside Kabul. Although everyone participating at the meeting asked him to stop the war immediately, he insisted that he would continue fighting for as long as Dostum's militas and the communists were allowed to remain in the government. When it was my turn to speak, I told him that if he was accusing the Kabul government of collaborating with the Uzbek militia of Dostum, then why was he together with Commander Jabbar Khan and his militia? After all, Jabbar Khan even had been awarded the title 'hero' or Qahraman by the communists! Mawlawi Khujandi told him that the communist administration of Helmand was headed by two puppet communist figures, Khanu and Allah Dad, both of whom supported Hekmatyar. They had both martyred scores of great mujahedeen. He suggested that Hekmatyar would do better to either rid his own party of the communists within, or should stop insisting that the Kabul administration do so. He should not make it a pretext, we said, for fighting against the Kabul government. Mr Hekmatyar didn't have a convincing answer for us and just said that he would surrender all these people to an Islamic court once established.

After the short rule of Hazrat Sibghatullah Mujaddidi, the six-month term of Burhanuddin Rabbani began. This period was the beginning of the war and of Kabul's destruction. The civil war worsened day by day. Burhanuddin Rabbani was so unfaithful to the mujahedeen that he did not look down and was unwilling to step aside once he took power.

We went to Kabul for a second time when the situation in Kandahar was worsening. There were different rulers in every corner. There was a war going on between Turan Ismael and Sufi Jabbar. There was a war between Turan Ismael and the people of Shindand over some Pashtu and Farsi language issues. When we reached Kabul, Ustad Burhanuddin Rabbani's interim administration's time was over, but he did not seem willing to leave power. So he gathered together some people who were connected to him and got their votes.

The clerics who had come to Kabul became very upset, particularly Abdullah Zakiri. We met with the clerics and talked to Ustad Burhanuddin Rabbani about the situation in general. We advised him that the Kandahar administration should be made up of great and capable mujahedeen in order to bring some peace of mind to the war-shattered nation there. He made a simple meaningless promise that was never fulfilled.

Before we came to Kabul, a delegation from our Council went to talk with Turan Ismael. We had hoped to get his agreement. Our delegation met with Wazir Akhund, who was a great mujahed, and Faqir Ahmad Khan in Shindand and then we were able to meet with Turan Ismael as well. Though he promised to help

in any way he could, he did nothing practical. It might have been because he was in power and head of the south-western zone, so he just didn't want to see an independent mujahedeen administration or power in Kandahar. After the trip to Herat, we went to Farah and talked to the key people in power there, however they were connected to Turan Ismael and did not want to join with us or cooperate. The public started electing representatives for the Council of Haal wa Aqd [12]. The people in our district again selected us as representatives for the council, so we headed to Kabul again. The Kabul Intercontinental was chosen as the place for the Council's participants to stay. We thought that the council would be the beginning of a period of comfort, construction and peace for the poor nation, and that it would take a fair decision about the country's leader, and that all jihadi leaders would be eligible for candidacy.
This was all just a dream. Burhanuddin Rabbani didn't allow anyone else to nominate themselves. Mawlawi Mohammad Nabi announced that he would come to Kabul and nominate himself as a candidate in the Council, but Rabbani (together with Sayyaf) held the Council's meeting before the scheduled date. People who were from the Kandahar administration participated in the election, but our council did not let its members vote and we did not show up at the hall where the Haal wa Aqd Council was meeting because such councils bring people to disunity and destruction instead of stability and construction.

It was the same story for the other provinces. Only those who were already picked used their votes and the real representatives of the people were not given any opportunity to express their views. The consequences of the symbolic council became known to the public and to the internationals. It did not offer anything except more hardships for the people of Afghanistan. Still, after witnessing the problems of the public in Kandahar, we informed Burhanuddin Rabbani of the shortcomings and problems of his Kandahar administration. The louder we made our voices, however, the more Rabbani turned a blind eye to us. Our council was slowly getting weaker and weaker financially as the government only was providing funds for those in the administration. Our fronts, the Taliban and the other real mujahedeen, struggled economically.

REMARKS

Kandahar's mujahedeen had good and bad features. The mujahedeen in the Taliban fronts and those fronts connected to them were very virtuous and well-behaved people. Almighty Allah's satisfaction, the victory of religion and the independence of the homeland were their only objectives. Other than these things, they would not even eat grapes from orchards when they were hungry during the jihad unless they had received permission from the owner.

The real mujahedeen were always in a bad way, financially. Most of the times they operated from money they collected as charitable donations. We had assigned two groups to collect charity money, led by Mullah Eshaqzai and Mullah Baran Akhund respectively. They would ask those praying in the mosque and everybody would give 10, or 20 or 50 or 100 Afghanis.
Our condition was not at all comparable to the mujahedeen who were being funded by the jihadi parties based in Peshawar. They were very well-equipped and received lots of money. Still, our mujahedeen performed their jihad bravely while bearing hunger, thirst and several other problems and destitution. Our mujahedeen were closely unified and always took the offensive on the battlefield. When the invading Russians' or the puppet government's military force came to an area and a group of mujahedeen would engage them, the mujahedeen of other areas would attack from multiple sides in order to distract the enemy from focusing on just one area. This tactic always worked and benefited the mujahedeen.
I mentioned that there were both good and bad people. Yes, unfortunately among those committed mujahedeen, there were dirty faces as well who did not even care about the Red Army's invasion, the destruction of villages and houses, martyrs, poor immigrants, widows or orphans. Those people took advantage of the holy name of jihad. They were involved in robberies and even entered into deals with the puppet government just to get some money.
By that time, especially after the embarrassing defeat of the Russians and the puppet government, those bad actions, cruelty and looting became public and well-known. People's property, honour and families were not safe. Everyone had set up

checkpoints on the main roads and highways and they would rob the passengers passing by under different names.

The people were in a very bad condition and the government was in the hands of the ignorant. If someone went to an institution to solve a case, the person in charge of the office would take a small round coin-shaped rock and made one side of it wet and left the other dry. He would ask both parties which side they wanted and then he would flip the stone in the air. Whichever side came out on top would determine the winner. That was what our courts and their decision-making process was like!

The people were miserable and they lived in horror. There were several systems in each corner of the country. Each group had set up a *patak* or checkpoint to loot the public and businessmen. Ethnic, religious, sectarian and regional wars were to be found all over the country. Hundreds of innocent people were being killed every day. Cities, villages, hospitals and other public institutions were destroyed and the cruel horror reached a peak. The youth were addicted to narcotics, gambling and other vices, and they were neglecting their education.

Life was difficult for people, and there was no trust for anyone. Love and brotherhood were replaced by hatred and hostility. In short, this was a period where the mujahedeen were defamed and when they lost their good name. The Westerners and the neighbours of Afghanistan were happy about that. According to the policy of divide and rule through the spread of corruption, they were busy. All of this was a plot by our sworn enemies against this Muslim nation, Islam, the holy blood of two million people that was shed on the path of Allah, as well as our widows and our orphans.

At that time, all those holding power in Kandahar started to collect more and more money regardless of who it was coming from or how it was being collected. Personal property was seized, and businessmen and the public were in trouble and had to pay money to all the *pataks* that were spread all over. Even if a poor ordinary citizen bought just a bag of flour for his family, he would be robbed or see his money extorted in some way. The public was in serious trouble and face the worst possible conditions. Their patience was running out. The central government did not have any control over the country aside for a few districts inside Kabul city where war, corruption and looting were happening as well. There was a war between Hekmatyar's *Hizb-e Islami*, Rabbani's *Jamiat*, Massoud's *Shura-ye Nazar*, Dostum's Gelimjan milita, Sayyaf's *Ittehad-e Islami* and the people of *Hizb-e Wahdat*. Those wars even spread out to other provinces.

The government administrations in the big cities were full of corruption and cruelty. In short, this nation was read to see a national uprising and wanted some kind of leadership around which all Afghans would gather together and solve their problems and put an end to the interference of outside interference, most of which was coming from our neighbours.
As the centre of southern Afghanistan, Kandahar has played a significant role in changing the country. Just as it had corrupt leaders at that time, there were also real and committed mujahedeen and Taliban as well. Most mujahedeen and Taliban had a very high standard of virtue and conduct for all their affairs, including their battles together. They also had a transparent court operating solely on the holy Islamic shari'a rules. This helped prevent corruption, and regardless of which party you were affiliated with, everyone obeyed the rulings and decisions of this court. *Huduud* and *qisas* were implemented throughout the period of jihad. The Taliban fronts in Kandahar were so united that people weren't even able to distinguish between the different groups. Organised Taliban fronts existed only in Kandahar. At any rate, it was necessary to end the ongoing crisis in the country and to end the corruption, immorality and cruelty. No other group could work to achieve this great goal because they were the only mujahedeen were not involved in these bad things. When the Taliban raised their voices for the first time, they were warmly welcomed and the public committed to any kind of assistance that was required.

THE TALIBAN'S MOVEMENT AGAINST THE EXTENDED PATAKS

During the final days of the puppet Najibullah government, I went with my Taliban mujahedeen from Pashmol to Arghandab. We visited the Mahalajat mujahedeen there and had a meeting with them to talk about the situation in Kandahar and to brainstorm hot to get rid of the *pataks*. In the end, all the mujahedeen agreed to destroy the *pataks*. We decided to work in an organised manner, in small groups consisting of a leader and their security. We were committed to destroying all of the *pataks* and ensuring security.

THE TALIBAN'S FIRST FIGHT AGAINST THE PATAKS

We first approached the *pataks* in Khwaja Malik area and fortunately managed to remove it without any fighting at all, through negotiation. The *patak* in Rubat area was taken down and the people manning it were killed. They had taken a woman by force as she was travelling through. They had kept her with them, and we released her. There was another *patak* at Khas Rubat area, which we removed as well. The *pataks* at Trang and Walduz areas were also removed. At that time, most of the *pataks* were located on the road leading to Pakistan, because that was the route that most vehicles took, especially trucks laden with goods. Once those *pataks* were removed, security was ensured and the public was very happy and satisfied with what had happened.

THE SECOND FIGHT OF THE TALIBAN AGAINST THE PATAKS

As time passed, some malicious people once against set up *pataks* to rob the people; they started to pose a threat to the security of the area again. Commander Abdul Raziq's mujahedeen — most of whom were Taliban led by Mullah Akhtar Mohammad Akhund — attacked Mullah Fateh's *patak* in the Arghestan area. The head of the Taliban group was martyred during the fight and people in the *patak* were also killed.

Meanwhile, Mullah Mohammad Ghaus Akhund, Mullah Nuruddin Turabi, Mullah Mohammad Rabbani and some others came to my house to discuss this issue. The mujahedeen demanded one thing, and that was to remove all the *pataks* from Kandahar and some other provinces as well. Some of those gathered didn't want to do this work in other provinces, however, fearing the hostility of other [local] mujahedeen groups and members of the public. At any rate, the Taliban had always wanted to fight against vice and provide a safe living environment for the public.

THE THIRD FIGHT OF THE TALIBAN AGAINST THE PATAKS

A third clash between the Taliban and the *pataks* was led by Mullah Mohammad Omar Akhund. A *patak* called Saleh in Pashmol was removed. This chain continued and new people joined up with the movement every day. After a while, the number of people in the movement became very large and the fight spread across from the borders of one province and moved to other parts of the country.

With the support of the public, the Taliban were finally able to eliminate the armed groups and the warlords. They took over most parts of the country including Kabul and founded a real Islamic system across all of Afghanistan. The reasons for the Taliban's victory had many reasons. Firstly, the Taliban had several organised fronts in Kandahar like my front. Most of my mujahed friends — like Mullah Mohammad Akhund, the Taliban's chief military commander; Mawlana, the Taliban minister of commerce; Mawlawi Mohammad Wali, the Taliban minister for the promotion of virtue and the prevention of vice; Hafiz Mohibullah, the Taliban minister of Hajj and religious affairs; Dr Obaidullah; Mohammad Lal; Gul Bandu Akhund; Mullah Mohammad Hassan Akhund, the governor of Kandahar during the Taliban's rule; Hajji Hayatullah known as Hajji La — and many more joined up with the Taliban movement.

The second large front was that of Commander Abdul Raziq, including the late Mullah Mohammad Rabbani, the Taliban ministers' council chief; the martyred Mullah Yar Mohammad, the Taliban governor of Herat; and Mullah Mohammad Ghaus, the Taliban minister of foreign affairs; along with many other mujahedeen. The head of the large front was Mullah Shireen Akhund and that included the martyred Mawlawi Abdul Hanan and Mullah Abdul Haq alongside other mujahedeen.

The fourth front was that of Mullah Hajji that included martyr Mullah Burjan Akhund, Mullah Hassan Akhund and other mujahedeen. The fifth front was Mullah Mohammad Sadiq Akhund's front that included several brave mujahedeen. I can name Mullah Abdul Salam Zaeef, Taliban ambassador to Pakistan, and Mullah Obaidullah Akhund, the Taliban minister of defence, as being two prominent members of this front.

After the Taliban movement started, most of these fronts joined up along with their mujahedeen and made all their equipment and resources available. Another reason for the quick victory of the Taliban movement was that Talibs from near and far madrassas joined up upon hearing their voice and helped them. Also, the Taliban's fronts had a good reputation during the jihad and the public had a high level of trust in them. The mujahedeen in those fronts were known for their good behaviour, trustworthiness, virtue and sympathy. For these reasons, the Taliban welcomed the Taliban everywhere, and this led to their victory around the country.

THE TALIBAN: A BRIEF INTRODUCTION

The Taliban had remained unbiased to a large extent. Although the new Taliban movement came into existence through the efforts of influential former Taliban figures (along with some new people), they were mostly committed mujahedeen who had performed jihad solely for their satisfaction and for almighty Allah, the victory of Islam and for the independence of the homeland. They did not have any interest in a structure or organisation like the political parties and those kinds of activities. They did not take sides according to the parties they had been affiliated with during the jihad. Allah awarded them with virtue on account of their knowledge and this was not new for them. There were people whose virtue I previously mentioned, such that they wouldn't even eat grapes from people's orchards when they were hungry and would not touch public wealth and property unless they had the permission of the owner. Those mujahedeen were known faces in the country and they had stayed out of the civil war. Away from the battlefield, they did not consider themselves entitled to punish or kill anyone without the decision of a shari'a-based court.

The Taliban were expert in military operations and jihadi affairs to a high degree. They had participated in hundreds or thousands of operations in which they acted according to the shari'a. They would divide the spoils of war equally according to the shari'a. They were content with very simple and humble lives. They passed their days eating very simple food. They never wasted their ammunition and weapons and tried their best not to incur unnecessary expenses from the Beit ul-Maal [13].

They did not seize the public institutions, nor did they fill their pockets from the Beit ul-Maal or expect gold or silver to be given to them. They hated those who engaged in vice and who had *pataks* under the guise of the title 'mujahedeen'.

One of the negative characteristics of the Taliban was that they didn't give a single chance to any of the jihadi leaders, even those who were committed, faithful and accepted by the public. They didn't allow them to get close to the Taliban; in fact, many commanders and mujahedeen found their lives became more difficult. The Taliban should have differentiated between good and bad and should have brought the good ones into the fold. The bad ones, they should have been punished following the decision of a shari'a-based court. In this way, they could have earned support from all over Afghanistan and founded a sustainable Islamic democratic government. Indeed, there is a well-known Pashto proverb that says, "you can't find the flower without the thorn."

WHO WAS AMIR UL-MU'MINEEN MULLAH MOHAMMAD OMAR MUJAHID?

Mullah Mohammad Omar Mujahed was a good mujahed. He had fought against the Russians and he lost one of his eyes during the war. Mullah Mohammad Omar Mujahed was with one of the fronts that were united with us. His front was affiliated with Harakat-e Enqelab-e Islami. Their front was headed by Faizullah Akhundzada who was Noorzai by tribe and very virtuous. He would wear clothes whose material was manufactured by the Gulbahar company and would wear a white turban made of khasa. His mujahedeen were mostly Taliban and he had some clerics with him on his front as well.

During the later part of the jihad, Mullah Mohammad Omar Mujahed — along with twenty-five other mujahedeen — became upset with Faizullah Akhundzada. At that time, their base was in Sangisar (part of Maiwand district). After he separated, he remained in Sangisar. At the time of the split, Mullah Abdul Ghani (known as Mullah Barader) went with Mullah Omar. The new group was affiliated with Harakat-e Enqelab-e Islami as well, and while they were short on weapons their fighters were very religious people and good mujahedeen. Their experience of the jihad was good as well, and they were willing to attempt everything. The mujahedeen respected him and followed him. The administration in 1994 was temporary, so he chose an acting minister of the ministries. This indicates that he was thinking to include other people in the government later on and not to make it just for the Taliban. It was an interim administration in a time of war, one without political knowledge. The problem was that the administration valued its own people over the nation or the well-known mujahedeen. I knew this from the fighters in our front who were always together with me and believed that commitment and knowledge/talent were both required. If someone had talent but no commitment, it wouldn't work, and vice versa.

WHY DID THE TALIBAN RISE UP?

The ongoing crisis, the different rulers for every few kilometres of the country, the civil war for power, the *pataks* and the rule of the warlords, the cruelty and the injustice, and the lootings and the robberies reached a peak. I explained the details of this in the previous pages. All these things encouraged the Taliban to take a stand against those miseries. They had to rise and take up arms to achieve their goal of eliminating cruelty and the cruel people and to protect the oppressed.

At the beginning, the Taliban first took action against the *pataks*. They fought against them and eliminated all of them. They never intended to take over the entire country and collapse the government. They didn't even think about moving on to other provinces and didn't realise that their would be so much public enthusiasm for them once they started.

Once the Taliban removed the *pataks* and discovered the public's support, they changed their original intention and decided to conduct extensive operations and to take over the government. They displayed this intention by first conducting large-scale operations in Kulak and Sulghi areas of Kandahar. They eliminated the *pataks* in those two areas and quickly managed to capture Kandahar City.

That victory further strengthened their morale and they became more competent in their combat skills. The Taliban were able to capture Zabul, Helmand and Uruzgan provinces in a very short time. The Taliban's speedy progress amazed people inside and outside the country. The Taliban captured most of the southern, south-western and south-eastern provinces quickly. Those swift battles, however, caused casualties on both sides. The Taliban was at the gates of Kabul by this point and they set up front lines in Maidan Shahr (Wardak) and Charasyab (Logar). The war to take the capital continued when the Taliban headed to the east and captured Nangarhar, Kunar, Laghman and Nuristan provinces. Remnants of the puppet government and the Shura-ye Nezar were defeated after a long fight and the Taliban entered Kabul. The Taliban suffered heavy casualties in this battle and the military chief, Mullah Burjan, was even martyred.

The Taliban didn't retreat, though, and they got rid of all of the armed groups that had been fighting for three years in Kabul and that had ruined the city and killed tens of thousands of innocents.

The Taliban established an Acting Council for the government. The armed groups that had been expelled from Kabul escaped to the north of the country and the Taliban chased them down. After capturing Parwan, Kapisa and Baghlan provinces, the Shura-ye Nazar militias wandered in the mountains and headed to Panjshir. The Taliban did not include any other groups as part of the Taliban into the mix of the Acting Council members.

They continued to move forward in northern Afghanistan. When they approached Balkh province, General Abdul Malik dishonestly offered to help them and to join with them. The Taliban made a huge mistake when they agreed to trust that country-selling communist. The Taliban sent unarmed delegations there without proper planning.

Thousands of Talibs waited there in a disorganised manner without a plan. Although some knowledgable leaders informed the Taliban's leadership — and the Amir ul-Mu'mineen — of the situation, the Taliban were certain they had everything under control. Unfortunately, General Malik succeeded in his malicious plot. Thousands of Talibs and their fellow mujahedeen were martyred on the first day. In addition, thousands of them were arrested and later martyred brutally in the Dasht-e Laili desert and in the wells of Sheberghan.

Those martyrs were all Talibs, mujahedeen and saintly youths.

Those bad and bitter moments have been recorded in the history of Afghanistan. Some of my relatives were among those who were martyred. May Allah punish those who were behind those bloody and inhumane actions in this world and in the next. Only a few of the hostages were released after enduring many hardships and problems. On this issue, I can only say that there were those among the Taliban who were not prepared to act properly and who would not think deeply about their actions and that is why almighty Allah imposed such a test on them and created so many problems.

At that time I came to Kabul together with Mullah Abdul Salam Zaeef and some other mujahedeen. Zaeef was my fellow from the time of jihad and he respected me greatly as someone older than him. May almighty Allah award him honour in this world and the next. I was warmly welcomed. After much insistence from Mullah Obaidullah Akhund and Nuruddin Turabi, I ended up taking responsibility for the fronts that extended in the Maidan Wardak circle ranging from Jalrez, Jalga, Jaghato and Chak districts.

I remained as head of the mujahedeen in that area for a year and then went home. After that I wasn't involved in the affairs of government any more because I wasn't interested in power. The Taliban's Islamic Emirate ruled 95% of the country for a few years. America and its allies created the September 11 incident in 2001 and took the presence of al-Qaeda as an excuse and prepared a major invasion of Afghanistan. In order to mount a military assault against Afghanistan, the US and its allies needed help on the ground. That was when the Northern Alliance welcomed the US and coalition forces into their areas. In the end, the American forces entered in northern Afghanistan with the direct support of the Northern Alliance and took the Afghan capital and major cities following heavy bombing and the firing of long-range missiles.

Afghanistan had not yet recovered from the miseries it had suffered following the defeat of one superpower and the civil war that followed, when it was attacked by another global superpower. Military forces from many countries of the world rushed to Afghanistan. The Taliban not only suffered heavy casualties in all corners of the country, but they were stuck in the northern parts and once again were hunted by the savage cruel people. Thousands were martyred, and thousands were martyred by Dostum and his ruthless militias after the Taliban were invited to surrender.

Those mass killings are dark spots in the contemporary history of the country. It was mostly Taliban who were stuck in Kunduz. Apparently, the Taliban leaders had talked with the leaders of the Northern Alliance, and with General Dostum, about the surrender of those Taliban and they were promised that the Taliban wouldn't be harmed. Accordingly, the Taliban leaders ordered their forces to surrender to General Dostum and that in that way they would remain safe.

Some were martyred immediately upon surrendering, and the rest — maybe as many as 12,000 — were taken in containers to Sheberghan and Mazar-e Sharif. Some were martyred on account of the poor conditions inside the containers due to the lack of oxygen, and the rest were martyred in very poor conditions inside the containers and because the oxygen ran out. The rest were martyred under different pretexts after they reached their destinations. The videos and news of those heart-rending incidents were published by different media outlets around the world.

Some of the Taliban who surrendered themselves to the Northern Alliance were then handed over to the Americans and illegally taken outside the country to spend years in Guantánamo and other prisons. Some of those people are still being held there. May Allah relieve them of this torture and may Allah grant their families and loved ones patience.

Karzai's government was established in Afghanistan after the US and coalition forces' invasion and the country was divided into two parts — north and south — according to the two languages, Dari and Pashto. At that time, a small number of Talibs were still being held by Dostum and there were some Northern Alliance prisoners in Taliban areas. It would have been good for them to be exchanged at the same time. Unfortunately, Karzai released all the Northern Alliance prisoners from Kandahar prison while Dostum kept the Taliban prisoners, who were later released after their families bribed some officials.

THE TALIBAN'S PUBLIC BEHAVIOUR

The Taliban were very humble people who led very simple lives. Most of them — especially those who were committed Talibs and who had some knowledge — were very virtuous and would not betray the movement. Those who were stationed in government institutions were very committed to their duties and would take care of the work of the people very quickly.

If someone in a government institution didn't do the work that they were supposed to on behalf of the people then there was a place for them to report this. There was no corruption at all. If anyone was found taking a bribe then when caught the Taliban would blacken their face and take him around in public.

The people mostly dealt with the Taliban's judges. This might be true for other countries as well, but during the Taliban's time the court decisions were made very quickly. They would not send plaintiffs away and they wouldn't take bribes. Of course, there were some people provoked by foreigners among the Taliban who would crack down on the former mujahedeen. Those were mostly new and young Taliban and very few of them were from the older generations. Those were not virtuous people and they collected so much wealth. They now have fancy houses abroad and the Taliban leadership was not happy with their actions.

Meanwhile there were also those among the Taliban who could barely meet their own basic financial needs and who had no access to health services, but who would never consider dipping into the Beit ul-Maal for their own purposes. In their offices they had simple furniture and wouldn't even sit on chairs. They were living the village life, sitting on mattresses around the edge of the room as was common in many parts of Afghanistan. They ate the same food as any other family and their equipment was simple as well, just as if they were living in the desert. They didn't change their clothes all the time and remained with their simple ways as before. They didn't change their clothes to go to work. They didn't wear suits and only wore *shalwar qamis*, traditional Afghan clothes. They weren't embarrassed by wearing old clothes and consider a turban one of their only required items. They didn't let people with shaved faces or long hair work together with the Taliban. They all grew their beards and the young men who didn't have beards weren't allowed to work together with the Taliban. Even a leader or a minister would travel using public transportation despite having a good car.

THE TALIBAN'S MILITARY CIRCLE

The Taliban military groups were very obedient. They would listen to their commanders even though they weren't drawing a salary. They had joined the Taliban voluntarily and there were very few places where people had to be drafted to make up the numbers. The volunteer forces did not approve of those who had been drafted. The military had good relations with the public and were very good at fighting. Wherever they were headed somewhere they would capture the place and that's why they were able to take Afghanistan very quickly. Nobody could resist them. Their weapons were old ones left over from the jihad time.

The military fighters would not travel home during the jihad and would mostly be away from home. Their leaders had so much control over them that they would do anything they asked. When Mullah Mohammad Omar Akhund ordered a commander to put down his weapons and stop fighting, he would do it without any argument. There was a military court for military crimes where they could try cases without delay. The Taliban had good discipline in their military affairs and observed the shari'a law very strictly.

SECURITY DURING THE TALIBAN TIME

I can't recall many murders in the city or desert during the Taliban time. If someone broke the law then he or she would be punished according to the shari'a and *huduud* would be carried out on him/her. Security was so good that a person could carry millions in cash from one place to another for business and nobody would dare rob him.

Let me mention that I was incarcerated in the NDS (National Directorate of Security) facility. At that time, I was robbed (through deception) by senior officials of that department. I told everybody about it at the time but it didn't do any good for me and I didn't get my money back. There was no looting, robbery, adultery, murder, bribery, bullying, cruelty or pederasty during the

Taliban's rule. The ministries at the time were not divided into groups and that is why when Amir ul-Mu'mineen wanted to replace a minister he didn't face any problems doing so.

THE TALIBAN'S PRISONS AND DETENTION CENTRES

There were very few inmates in the prisons during the Taliban time, mainly because there were no murders, robberies or other immoral actions that would require people to be jailed. They tried their best not to arrest people as political prisoners in the areas under their control. Even if they arrested someone, they would try to release him quickly in order to prevent the people becoming hostile with them.

There was even a jail for the young that was called the Corrections Centre. It included a madrassa and people would even bring their own children to the centre, asking us to hold them there and to teach them.

Hundreds of people were often arrested during the fighting, but they would then be released on the orders of the Minister of Justice, Nuruddin Turabi. Anyway, there were a few inmates and it was easy to get released. There is a Pashto proverb that says: "The cruel person has many prisoners." For example, Hujjaj, son of Yusuf, had imprisoned thousands of the companions of the Prophet. And generous people have a lot of money.

I should add that during the Taliban's rule, there were some non-political inmates being held in one block of Pul-e Charkhi and the rest of the blocks were empty.

SAFETY OF PUBLIC PROPERTY DURING THE TALIBAN TIME

It was impossible to seize the property of other people during the Taliban time and even government land could not be redistributed. During Rabbani's government, our mujahedeen were given around seventy marketplaces to be built on government land. Some were built and others were not when the Taliban came. Even though those mujahedeen were part of the Taliban leadership, they were not allowed to use those markets. The Taliban stopped giving out registered ownership documents to prevent people from forging documents for someone else's property.

By the end, after they had more power around the country, they resumed registering land ownership documents in the courts. Now that the Taliban are gone, the personal property of people is often seized and no government land is left. Forged documents have been made for personal property. The Taliban had great support from the public because they had come with the support of the public. The people cooperated a lot for the arrest of robbers and for the ending of other vices, because the Taliban themselves were not corrupt. They would listen to the complaints of the oppressed. They stopped cruel people from their actions. The cruel either changed what they were doing, or they left the country. That is why nobody had any problems carrying large amounts of cash from one place to the other. The public also obeyed the Taliban and an indication of this was that when the Taliban banned poppy cultivation, nobody grew it any more.

PROMOTION OF VIRTUE AND THE PREVENTION OF VICE IN AFGHANISTAN

The Ministry for the Promotion of Virtue and the Prevention of Vice has recently come under a lot of criticism. The minster of this administration was one of my mujahedeen during the jihad period. His virtue and fear of Allah was known to me and he was a knowledgeable person. His name was Mawlawi Mohammad Wali and he was from Siachoy village of Panjwayi district of Kandahar province. He was martyred in the bombings. Two of his brothers were martyred in the war against the Russians on our front.

There are a few reasons for the criticisms of the Ministry for the Promotion of Virtue and the Prevention of Vice. There were some negative points, but also some positive things. This kind of institution was not new in the Islamic world and it has been active in Arab-speaking countries for a long time. It was new in Afghanistan, however, and had strict rules. Those strict rules seemed to be difficult for Afghans to follow.

The minister was also not especially professional, slowly starting and gradually introducing things until people became used to the new rules. An indication of his unprofessionalism was that he set up *pataks* for prayers and would make everyone pray

regardless of whether they were sick or hadn't even done their ablutions. Many people (including myself) told him that they should perform their duties like the Saudis do, only asking the shopkeepers to shut their shops during prayer time and guiding people to perform their prayers. Other people in the city usually had to work with the shopkeepers and when the shops were closed they would come and perform the prayers.
In some provinces, uneducated people were assigned to this administration. Most of the things that the Ministry for the Promotion of Virtue and the Prevention of Vice implemented were necessary, but they should have been introduced gradually. Anyway, the ministry was good from an Islamic perspective and Muslims need it, and there is no question about whether it should have existed in the first place as some people have said.

ARAB MUJAHEDEEN IN AFGHANISTAN

Arab youths entered the Afghan jihad as soon as it first started against the Russians. They not only performed jihad, but also provided financial assistance. The Arab states also believed that the Afghan jihad needed to be strengthened, and so those states provided financial support as well.
Meanwhile, those states didn't prevent their Arab mujahedeen from coming to Afghanistan. The Arabs who performed the jihad in Afghanistan were very pure and good people. Their virtue was high as I knew them well and there were many Arab mujahedeen with us. I honoured and appreciated their work and would even give them our weapons when they wanted to go to another front. In terms of bullets, I had directed the mujahedeen not to refuse the Arab mujahedeen bullets when they asked for them. For these reasons, they were happy with me and wherever I went to conduct operations, Arab mujahedeen from other bases would also go with me. I always respected them as guests and cared for them.

Once I went to Zabul and many Arab mujahedeen came as well. If any Arab mujahed wanted to go home or to Pakistan and couldn't afford to do so, I paid for them. They supported our fronts very well and I even got funds for other fronts from them. Many of them were martyred and wounded, but their fellow countrymen would not get upset. Whenever any of them was martyred they would bury him at the same place and not transfer them to a different place according to the shari'a.

The Arab mujahedeen had a big influence on the Arab aid agencies like the Red Crescent, al-Jannat ul-Da'wa, Hay'at ul-Eghsa and so on. Some countries like Iraq and Libya didn't allow their citizens to come to Afghanistan for jihad and would imprison those who tried to come. In fact, those countries were providing assistance to the communist government. Still, their mujahedeen would come secretly to Afghanistan and would sometimes have to stay for a long time. Famous jihadi figures among the Arabs included: Abdullah Azzam, Osama bin Laden, Abdullah Maharib (who was martyred in Kandahar) and Sheikh Abdul Majid Zendani and some others through whom the mujahedeen received so much support.

Some Arab mujahedeen stayed in Afghanistan. Osama bin Laden, Ibn Sheikh from Libya, Abu Mus'ab al-Zarqawi (who later went to Iraq) and some other Arabs who couldn't return to their countries stayed in Afghanistan during the Rabbani government's time. Later on, when the Taliban came, they joined together with the Taliban.

There were even Arab mujahedeen who had married in Bosnia who then moved to Afghanistan with their families. The Taliban respected them as they did during the jihad time. They were treated as guests in Afghanistan. Those Arabs did not even think to use Afghan soil for their benefit or to harm other countries. Meanwhile, the Taliban wouldn't let them do so.

There were three types of Arabs in Afghanistan. One group was led by Ibn Sheikh. Another group, the largest, was led by Osama bin Laden. And the third group was a charitable organisation called al-Wafa. They got married with their own people and didn't deal with Afghans. When the Taliban government collapsed, the Arabs left the country via Jalalabad, Paktya, Spin Boldak and some other routes. Some of those Arabs were martyred in Takhtepul area.

There were some people who didn't show any sympathy towards those Arabs and didn't give them any kind of human rights. They martyred some injured Arabs in the Chinese Hospital in Kandahar. The Pakistani ISI acted very cruelly against their families and handed them over to the Americans after their arrest. One might ask what the Arab mujahedeen were doing in Afghanistan during the Taliban's government time. The answer is that the Arab mujahedeen always supported a holy group just as they had done so during the jihad against the Russians. They would fight against the enemy as they were doing in Chechnya and Bosnia. Their friendship was an indication of the Taliban's goodness. There is no doubt that the Taliban were a good people and god-fearing as well.

HOW DID MULLAH DADULLAH AKHUND RELEASE THE TALIBAN IN THE NORTH?

Mullah Dadullah Akhund was a great mujahed. I knew him personally very well as he spent ten years in our village. He lived there and grew up as a teenager in Mawlawi Akhtar Mohammad Agha's front. He was with us when the groups joined together. Whenever I sent Mullah Mohammad Akhtar Agha — who was head of the joint group — to a particular place, Mullah Dadullah Akhund would be selected as the head of the rest of the group. He managed to perform his duties very well. When the Taliban movement dominated Afghanistan, Mullah Mohammad Akhund was martyred in the early days. After him, Mullah Rahmatullah Akhund was the second person after Mullah Mohammad Omar and Mullah Dadullah was among those that followed. In my opinion, he did some great things.

When General Abdul Malik caused thousands of Taliban casualties and martyred them brutally in the north — arresting some of them, martyring them in prisons or beating them up and throwing them into wells dug by previous rulers — Mullah Dadullah didn't lose his morale. He gathered together some Taliban who had escaped to one place in the north, captured Baghlan and Kunduz very quickly and went forward until most northern provinces were captured and ground transportation to the north from Kabul was possible again. Aside from Badakhshan, all the other provinces were captured and Mullah Dadullah played a significant role in that.

The next time Mullah Dadullah was engaged in the north by the Americans, and when the Americans took over the north, the remaining Taliban refused to surrender to Dostum — who was a communist — because he had promised he would keep them safe and return them to their homes safely. It was wise that they didn't trust the enemy, though. Mullah Dadullah told me his story from that time. He said that he wasn't willing to surrender himself to Dostum as the relationship between them was one of force and power. As they were leaving, when someone asked them where they were going, he told them they were invited by Dostum while they kept their hands on their pistols at their sides. In some parts on the way back he had to walk and leave the cars they were driving. He had heard that the enemy had taken up positions on the highways for him, but he was then interviewed and said that he arrived in Kandahar. After that, Dostum's people stopped searching for him on the main roads and he managed to escape.

MY PERSONAL OPINION

From my point of view, it would have been better if the Taliban analysed the activities, successes and shortcomings of the previous governments and tried not to make the same mistakes. For instance, the interim communist government after the Saur coup sought to dominate the people through force and they appointed their own people in government offices around the country, but they never managed to win the support of the public. This is why those governments didn't last very long.

Also, the Islamic government of our neighbour, Iran, was a good example for the Taliban. Khomeini led the revolution and established a government that was led by clerics. His main reason for success was that he established a strong force called the Sipah-e Pasdaran, and this force had control over the entire country and nobody dared revolt. He appointed some people to important positions and left the rest of the government for the public. He created jobs and work opportunities for them and moved the country towards construction and development. That government has now completed forty years with the support of the public and it is still in place. People trust it and the country is well-constructed and developed in all fields. All their people are working and ready to sacrifice their heads to serve their government. This is because they are ruling with the love of the people. Therefore at that time, when Afghanistan was just coming out of a 30-year war and had just defeated a big dragon, it was impossible to just have the Taliban's govern-

ment and not include mujahedeen. If the Taliban wanted to have a sustainable government and keep peace and stability in the country, it would have beeen good if they had taken important institutions such as the military, courts and some others in their hands and then left the rest of the ministries and provincial administration for committed, good people. That would have made the public happy on one hand, and on the other hand their government would be sustainable for a long time.
If the Taliban had chosen the path of peace after the war, they could have increased their supporters and avoided destruction, death and casualties. Jihadi leaders such as Mohammadi, Khalis, Pir Saheb and Harzrat Saheb, who were not involved in the civil war, should have been invited along with other similar clerics to contribute to founding a strong and sustainable administration. That would have ensured the public's interest; however, this did not happen. Mujahedeen were paid no attention during the Taliban's rule. For example, if a family member was martyred while in Taliban lines, that family was exempted when more people were next drafted for wars. However, this rule did not cover families whose family members were martyred during jihad.

Also, it would have been much better if the Taliban stuck in the north during the American invasion were surrendered to the mujahedeen instead of to Dostum's militias, because Dostum's Gelimjam militia's cruelty and brutality were known as well as the sun in Afghanistan. It's possible that mujahedeen in the north would have treated Taliban detainees better than Dostum's militias did, or at least they would not have martyred them all. It's worth mentioning that one good aspect of the Taliban Islamic Emirate was tight security, the first need for society and for the implementation of shari'a laws.
During the Taliban's rule, the country was so safe that it couldn't be compared to any other country in the world. Pure Islamic shari'a dominated; *huduud*, *qisas* and other shari'a punishments were given by courts. Courts operated very transparently and were not influenced by other officials. Administrative corruption was not common at all. In one instance someone in Kandahar had received a bribe. They caught him immediately, blackened his face, put him in a car and drove him through the city so that everybody could see him getting punished for what

he had done, to make an example of him. They were very quick in governmental affairs; for example, if a minister or any other governmental official was to be changed, he would be replaced quickly after the issuing of the order and there was not even a minute's delay. Although most officials were not familiar with political and national governmental affairs, they were very committed and trustworthy people.

DIFFERENCES BETWEEN THE GOVERNMENTS THAT FOLLOWED THE COMMUNISTS

It is common for governments in Afghanistan to be dependent on a group, party or a movement and to keep the public and citizens in one corner and away from the government. Any group that takes over the power, it gives more power to people connected to it in order to maintain the power for themselves. From my point of view, such governments cannot impress the nation and Afghans are usually influenced this way. Therefore, it would be appropriate to trust the influential and virtuous people of all groups and share them in the government. The governments we have witnessed while having difference in terms of their strategies, religious observations and ruling, they all had a personal form.

Rabbani's government had countless gaps. Civil war went on in all corners of the country and outside the capital; all the districts and provinces were out of Kabul's control. Also, the courts were not operating in accordance with the Shari'a laws. Other mujahedeen groups were treated very badly. Not only were they deprived from playing a role in the government, but if they wanted to talk about their right to a share of the power in government then they could expect a fight about it.

The Taliban's Islamic Emirate had it's unique characteristics and gaps. Although it had a personal form and other groups were not given the opportunity to contribute, it operated according to the Holy Islamic shari'a and Islamic laws were carried out to a large extent. Security was very good and public property and honour were safe in all places that the Islamic Emirate controlled. The current Karzai-led administration is in its twelfth year of rule. The government only controls a very small area around the district centres and most positions are divided among two main groups. Nobody else can participate in the government. Instead of basing the system on the Islamic shari'a and other laws originating in Islam, it is founded upon the idea of Democracy. Administrative corruption, bribery, the exclusivity of power, bullying and the looting of public property that has no place in Islamic society or in the holy religion of Islam have reached peak levels. The foreigners dominate all government affairs and the foreign forces do whatever they want, whenever they want, without the knowledge of the Afghan government. Our justice, economy and other parts of our country are being built by foreigners. All these things call into question the independence of the country and the government.

AMERICA'S ATTACK ON AFGHANISTAN AND THE ARRIVAL OF THE COALITION FORCES

The head of Shura-ye Nazar, Ahmed Shah Massoud, was killed in a suicide attack by two Arab journalists in Bahauddin area of Takhar province on September 9, 2001. Just two days later, several attacks took place in different parts of America.

According to the Americans, around 3000 people were killed in those attacks. Americans hastily reacted and blamed everything on al-Qaeda. They also blamed the ruling government in Afghanistan, the Islamic Emirate, for hosting al-Qaeda. Along with its allies, America decided to attack Afghanistan to end the government and to root out al-Qaeda. They made it seem like al-Qaeda was a threat to international security and with this pretext they attacked Afghanistan from the sky and from the seas. America and her allies were very smart. They had learnt from the Russians' experience in Afghanistan. They spread fear about al-Qaeda among all the non-believers and their allies. It was just part of their pre-scheduled plans and interests for the region and for Afghanistan. The attack on al-Qaeda was just a pretext, because attacking such a small group with the militaries of over fifty powerful countries with the most modern equipment seems funny. America and the other westerners didn't help Afghans during the Russian invasion merely for the sake of Allah and the Islamic beliefs of Afghans. They didn't spend their money here to relieve the oppressed Afghan nation from the Red invading and colonising force. Their purpose was to end the Russian influence on Asian countries so that they could have carte blanche to behave as they wished in Asia themselves.

When the small number of empty-handed Afghans gained victory against the global superpower with the help of almighty Allah and the holy religion of Islam, unfortunately they still lacked some things. This was mainly the lack of a sympathetic, patriotic and hardworking leader. It was because of this that the civil war broke out. The government either didn't exist at all, or, where it did, its presence was patchy. It was at that moment when America picked Afghanistan as its geopolitical entry point. In order to come to Afghanistan, however, it needed an excuse for the international community and the people in the region. Al-Qaeda's presence here was like a gift for them, and so they needed to topple the Taliban government as well, since it was considered the host of al-Qaeda.

In addition to their international allies, America needed allies and friends in the region itself. After some research, they chose those gathered under the umbrella of the Northern Alliance. They gained access to Afghan soil by buying off the Northern Alliance. The Americans pounded the Taliban with the help of the Northern Alliance. They killed many of them; some important Taliban figures were arrested and others were forced to leave the country. This is how the Americans occupied Afghanistan and established a weak government made up of the Northern Alliance and some other groups. They are dominated by the infidels in the country, and everything is run based on their commands; nobody else has any power. The mujahedeen and all the other committed Muslims and capable individuals aren't able to take part in the government.

Although most of the mujahedeen remained inside Afghanistan, they weren't viewed as positively as the communists and the westerners. The Taliban were rejected out of question; they were expelled from the country and nobody wanted to negotiate with the Taliban at all.

One time, Mr Turabi (the former Taliban minister of justice) went and met with Gul Agha Shirzai, the governor of Kandahar at that time. He was assured that they could live freely without worries in Kandahar. However, when the Americans heard about this meeting, they announced that nobody had immunity. It was at that point that Mr Turabi and his fellows went to Pakistan. But people can make their own judgement as to whether the government has any power. Isn't the lack of independence clear?

SUMMARY

The circumstances when we were mujahedeen was quite strange. At the beginning, the mujahedeen were very poor and the jihadi parties also didn't have much. Even if they had something, they would give most of their money to their own people. Our fronts had nothing; we collected charitable donations to cover our jihadi expenses. Special groups were assigned to collect this money from the mosques. They would spread out their patu in mosques and people would contribute as much as they could. Some were able to give ten and others twenty. That money would then be gathered together and the mujahedeen would exist from that. The mujahedeen that were surviving from *zakat*, however, were in a better condition.

At that time, the mujahedeen were very pure and committed, and followed the rules of holy Islam. Islamic inspiration among Muslims reached its peak during the jihad, and they removed the love of women, children and this world from their hearts for the sake of martyrdom. That is why the mujahedeen were successful during this time.

The parties had significant resources and economic power, and the Pakistani government tried collecting aid for the Afghan mujahedeen. They started to put pressure on the jihadi parties to send enough supplies to the mujahedeen on the ground. A short time later, Pakistani officials started to pay attention to the mujahedeen and set up councils for them and provided weapons and other resources directly through those councils. Later, though, the Communist government made efforts to buy some mujahedeen. The loyalty and commitment to operations decreased; but those mujahedeen who hadn't made connections with the government continued their good operations.

Later on, the Taliban and their fellow mujahedeen were kept away from the administration. By that time, the aid from Pakistan had stopped and the government only provided support to those in the administration. The mujahedeen outside the administration were provided no support to cover their expenses. Our mujahedeen became truck drivers to earn money to pay for the expenses of those fighting inside Afghanistan.

There were two types of mujahedeen: the first group were in our front under the Taliban and our allies who were so close with us that they could not be distinguished from the mujahedeen of our front; the second group were ordinary mujahedeen with whom we collaborated only for big operations.

That is why the mujahedeen of the Taliban front and their allies were kept from any government administration after the fall of the Communists. The second group of mujahedeen had created a council and took control of the city. They did not like our mujahedeen and were mostly corrupt people. They couldn't follow through with the Taliban's restrictions on themselves. Also, when the Communists had handed over power to them, they had insisted that the Taliban be not allowed to share in power.

LIST OF OPERATIONS IN WHICH I PARTICIPATED

1. Tur Taaq front where the non-believers conducted operations against us
2. Our guerrilla operations in Kandahar city which were unprecedented at that time
3. Operations against a big force in Nagehan; the force came three times and we fought back strongly
4. Operations against soldiers in Arghandab
5. Attacks on Russian convoys when we were in Arghandab
6. Operations on the road at different times
7. Continuous operations in the city at different times
8. Our operations against the force in Mahalajat
9. Operations in Baba Saheb
10. Operations against Dala base
11. Operations in Shah Wali Kot district
12. Operations against forces in Pashmol at different times
13. Daily operations against convoys passing on the road in Charbagh area
14. Operations against the force in Charbagh when Lala Malang was martyred
15. Participating in Tirin Kot operations in Uruzgan
16. Conducting different types of attacks (missiles and face-to-face attacks) at the airport

17. Strikes of 122-type missiles at Kandahar airport
18. Hitting and downing a plane in Daman area and arresting the pilots
19. Big operations against Kandahar airport
20. Continuous attacks with dc mortar and the 122 missile against the airport
21. Two operations in Zabul
22. Operations in Shna Narai where the enemy attacked the mujahedeen's depots
23. Continuous operations in Panjwayi district at different times
24. Operations by our front went on in multiple locations at the same time. We had mine-planting groups — one of which was led by Mullah Lal Mohammad Akhund and another by Mullah Tur Akhund. Our base in Pashmol was always engaged in a fight with a force or would be gone somewhere else conducting operations. Charbagh base would always attack the Russian convoys; that group was led by Mullah Mohammad Akhund or Mullah Ahmad Lal Akhund. Another hub of our front was in Arghandab led by Sufi Mullah Qayyum Akhund. That group would fight in areas belonging to Arghandab district. Another base of ours was in Sabzi Kar led by Mullah Mohammad Hassan Rahmani, who was in charge of operations in the city.
25. Operations of the joint group led by Mullah Burjan in Mahalajat areas
26. Operations of the joint group led by Mawlana Abdul Raziq in the prison area

MY EMIGRATION: LEAVING THE HOMELAND FOLLOWING THE AMERICAN ARRIVAL

America and its allies attacked Afghanistan as they had promised. First, they conducted heavy attacks with long-range cruise missiles from the sea and from the air with B-52 bombers. They struck Kabul and other major cities that were controlled by the Taliban. Most cities didn't have any people because the explosions from the bombs and missiles were so big. People were forced to move to surrounding areas, and those who had more money emigrated to Pakistan. Although many friends and relatives recommended that I stay in Afghanistan and go to a safe location, I knew that it was usual for new regimes to mistreat those associated with the old governments. For this reason I preferred to leave. At the same time, America's activities in Afghanistan were an obvious invasion; they did not just simply come, they came bringing bloody war and mass murder.

I still had dreams of jihad on my mind, so I thought Pakistan would be a safe haven for myself and other mujahedeen who did not approve of the US invasion of Afghanistan. I did not know that Pakistan had two-faced policies and that Islam and brotherhood came after its own interests; that it preferred American slavery to the values of Islam. Anyway, I escaped to Pakistan and lived there while I received information about what was going on in Afghanistan. News of mass murders of Taliban in the north were very difficult to bear. When it became clear that Dostum and his militias had brutally killed thousands of Taliban and accused thousands of Pashtuns of being Taliban, capturing and killing them, I became very sad. Thousands of people were killed; many were suffocated inside containers and the rest died from torture, starvation and other hardships in prisons. What was very saddening was that Dostum and his militias were not the only people responsible. There were other people who called themselves Afghans, and also America and its allies, who considered themselves peaceful people who were here to end casualties and ensure security in this region. Nevertheless, they did not prevent the savage Dostum from martyring 25,000 innocent people. There was nobody at the time to speak up about human rights and prevent this terrible crime, the likes of which haven't been seen elsewhere in recent history. Not only Taliban, but also Pashtuns from villages, were taken out and killed en masse. Pashtuns must have been killed, because there weren't 25,000 Taliban in the north; there were estimated to have been only 12,000, far fewer than the 25,000 casualties.

In the blind bombardments and military operations of America and the coalition forces, many villages were ruined and large numbers of people were martyred across the country, especially in the south and the east. In addition, many people were taken out of their houses regardless of their innocence and, contrary to all Islamic and international laws, were taken to fierce prisons such as Guantánamo and Bagram without consulting with the government. The two-faced policy of Pakistan, who was first to recognise Taliban Islamic Emirate and would even help sometimes, but then took America and the West's side, was not tolerable either. Taliban and mujahedeen who had sought refuge in Pakistan were being arrested and handed to either the Afghan government or the Americans, or put in Pakistani prisons, which are worse than America's detention centres. They tortured detainees in various ways, and would dishonour greatly respected people. This was not acceptable to us and other mujahedeen who had always stood against cruelty and invasion. It was not a time to remain indifferent. Therefore we, along with committed mujahedeen brothers, established a movement called Jaish ul-Muslimeen. The objectives of Jaish ul-Muslimeen were staying informed of Afghanistan's condition, countering vice, promoting competence, and supporting and serving the oppressed nation of Afghanistan. Jaish ul-Muslimeen sought to conduct themselves according to the teachings of the Prophet (PBUH), "If any of you see a vice, he must change it with his hand, if he cannot do that, he should change it with his tongue and if he cannot do that either, he should hate the vice in his heart and that is the lowest degree of faith." Jaish ul-Muslimeen had peace talks in its agenda, in addition to armed fighting, and it was one of its primary goals to either gather, or become allies with, virtuous, patriotic and sympathetic Afghans. The prime objective of Jaish ul-Muslimeen was to unite the Taliban, mujahedeen and other religious and patriotic groups in the country. Jaish ul-Muslimeen did not have any personal enmity with any group and considered its supporters and opposing groups the same. They loved the jihad of the mujahedeen and respected it. The number of Jaish ul-Muslimeen members increased from day to day. We tried not to upset anybody and we kept Islamic moderation to a high extent. We tried our best to rescue others from casualties and choose ways that would ensure the safety of Afghan lives and honour so that nobody would oppose us.

THE ARREST OF THREE FOREIGNERS ACCUSED OF INTERFERENCE IN AFGHAN INTERNAL AFFAIRS

Three foreigners working for the United Nations were arrested on 28 October 2004 in Kabul. The captors of the three foreigners had good relations with Taliban Islamic Emirate during the

Taliban's rule. In addition to having good relations with the Taliban, they were indirectly in contact with Jaish ul-Muslimeen as well. It must be mentioned that their taking these hostages was driven by their Islamic beliefs and was not for personal benefit or obtaining money. When that happened, I was out of the country and did not know about it. The captors had contacted some Jaish ul-Muslimeen members and told them they wanted to be Jaish ul-Muslimeen members from that time on and that they wanted to announce the foreign hostages through us. Members of the council agreed with them and later announced that Jaish ul-Muslimeen had the three foreign UN employees in their custody.

At that time I was away from the area and learned about this incident after hearing the announcement. I tried to get more information about the incident. I had two main thoughts about the incident: one, I did not like foreigners and their interference in Afghanistan at all; secondly, since there were women among the hostages, and incarcerating women and causing them suffering contradicts Afghan traditions, I needed to be very careful and release the hostages as soon as possible. War was still raging in the country and the public hated foreigners, and had risen against them. Foreigners had killed many innocent Afghans and many other Afghans were suffering greatly, in contradiction with all international laws, in the foreigners' detention centres. That's why releasing the foreigners was not an easy option, and not free from risk. The only reason I was in a hurry to release them was the presence of women among them. The people who had taken those foreigners hostages were not our friends; meanwhile, those foreigners were employees of the UN and my personal point of view, and Jaish ul-Muslimeen policy, was to not harm United Nations employees. Nevertheless, the UN is not an independent organisation, and operates under the direction of a few powerful non-Islamic countries. It has never cared for Muslims but rather condemned them in all corners of the world. However, when non-believers have risen against Muslims or have been cruel to Muslims, the UN has remained silent. The UN was established by powerful non-believing countries to threaten Muslims and justify killing them through this organisation. They have always violated the rights of Muslims and Muslim countries by imposing sanctions on them under one or another pretext. In short, I did not want the foreign women spending time with strangers in captivity, but releasing them was out of my control. If I'd had control over releasing them, I would have done it without any delay and would not have left those women in custody with strangers.

I don't approve of Afghan and Pakistani officials, because foreigners arrested Aafia Siddiqui in Pakistan and transferred her to Bagram, but then announced that she had been arrested in the Ghazni province of Afghanistan. Afghan officials didn't have the zeal to sympathise with her, nor did Pakistani officials help her. Even then, the non-believers were not satisfied and took her to America. It is sad to be Muslim and not sympathise with a Muslim woman in the hands of non-believers. That has never been my view, is not my view now and will not be in future. With that mindset, I continued my efforts to release these foreigners even though some people criticised me for this in our meetings. There were even some people who did not accept responsibility for arresting Aafia Siddiqui, and would even say that it was their right to arrest an honourable woman. Of course the Muslim nation of Pakistan rallied and demonstrated, but other Muslim countries kept their mouths shut. However, everybody blamed us for taking our hostages, despite knowing about our suffering. I was sure that God sees both the good and bad in us and that there will be a judgement day when it will be known who worked for God's sake and who worked for their personal benefit.

MY ARREST ON DECEMBER 4, 2004 IN KARACHI, PAKISTAN

The Pakistani government and its intelligence agency, ISI, were trying their best to arrest me. Many of my friends had informed me of this. The only reason that the Pakistani government and ISI wanted to arrest me was that I did not have a relationship with them that would benefit them in any way. They did not like people who would not listen to them and do as they were told. Many close friends recommended that I go into hiding or go to areas out of Pakistan's control to be safe. However, I did not pay much attention and continued to live as I always had. Sometimes, I would even drive to Karachi myself.

On November 25, 2004, I moved to Karachi. After three nights, on a Friday morning, I received a message from a high-ranking Afghan official, whose name I won't mention, asking me where I was at the moment. I told him that I was in Karachi, in my house. I had a guest who was on his way to Karachi; he asked me about this guest as well. He probably asked about the guest simply to avoid suspicion, but his main intention was to make sure that I was at home. About half an hour after the conversation, the Pakistan military, who are Muslims by name but even crueler than non-believers, entered my house without permission and attacked me ruthlessly. They didn't ask me to go with them, but rather, much like wolves who've caught a sheep, they started beating me in front of my children. Even though there was no need for it, they engaged in this infidels' action. In fact, their American bosses standing at the gate were better than them, because they were actually less savage and cruel than the Pakistanis. They beat me so badly that my face started bleeding. The worst thing of all was my sons and daughters crying and begging them not to beat their father. However, there was nobody among the attackers sympathetic enough to those innocent children to stop beating me. The beating on that bitter day did not hurt in comparison, and I did not even make any noise, but the crying of my innocent little sons and daughters made me very sad. Their screams will echo in my ears for a long time, and I will never forget it. Thankfully, everything is this world passes, be it happiness or grief, comfort or torture. All the hardships I went through at that time passed. May Allah keep us from having problems with our faith and religion and may Allah not make me so cruel as to not have mercy for children, as they had no mercy and didn't delay in beating me but in fact made it worse.

In short, they handcuffed me and put a black bag over my head and face. We went out and they pushed me into the car parked outside. They took me directly to the ISI and locked me in a dark jail. They treated me terribly from the beginning. I discovered later that the ISI headquarters were close to my house, but they actually drove into the city and turned back to their office to distract me.

DETAILS ABOUT THE ARREST OF THE THREE FOREIGNERS

On the day that those three UN employees were taken hostage, I was in my home in Karachi and was totally unaware of what was happening. I personally hadn't instructed anybody, nobody gave me information, nor did anyone seek my advice on the capture. I learned only via the media that Jaish ul-Muslimeen had taken three foreigners hostage. I usually followed up on news at night after I was done with other tasks. That night, I was surprised by the news. I immediately tried to find out who could have captured the hostages. I telephoned my friends, asked them and found out that the incident had taken place as I described earlier. This incident had taken place during Taliban rule and then some people had contacted members of Jaish ul-Muslimeen in my absence, had posed as Jaish ul-Muslimeen members and had asked to announce the hostages through the media. That was news to me and when I contacted high ranking Jaish ul-Muslimeen officials, they would not give me all the details. Now I can see that some members of the Taliban and Jaish ul-Muslimeen were involved in that incident, but why did the captors contact Jaish ul-Muslimeen and not the Taliban? The answer to this is that the Jaish ul-Muslimeen were very humble people, and that the captors tended towards Jaish ul-Muslimeen's ideology. Anyway, I did not approve of this incident at first, because it seemed unplanned and aimless to me. I told most of my friends that it would have been better if it had not happened. However, my friends said that the captors insisted they were not going away from Jaish ul-Muslimeen but rather respected Jaish ul-Muslimeen, because it had good strategy and peaceful policies, so they wanted to remain members of the organisation. They said that they would accept the Jaish ul-Muslimeen decision about the hostages. Ultimately we decided to release the hostages and pay the captors' expenses.

Although the captors had not obtained the approval of the organisation, we agreed to release the hostages while following Allah's direction and avoiding any negative response from the oppressed Afghan people. Mostly, the public supported the hostage taking, and we received several demands not to release the hostages. We received the same request from a small number of people working in the government as well. Finally, we decided to negotiate over thousands of innocent Taliban who were in the government's custody. Therefore, one group was assigned to negotiate an exchange with the government and foreigners and another group was assigned to get the approval of the captors and their associates. Although they agreed in face to face talks, the release of the hostages was still not in our power. Still, we needed to try our best to release the hostages as soon as possible, as the government would release Taliban detainees in exchange. For many reasons, we needed to be very careful; on the one hand we needed to get the approval of Afghans who did not favour the release, because most of them were against foreigners' interference in Afghanistan's internal affairs, and many were loyal to the religion and the country. We did not want to be spoken badly of by such committed people and lose our reputation. On the other hand, the loved ones of our fellow mujahedeen from the days of the jihad were in government detention, so they wanted us to exchange these foreigners for the release of their people, and they were right because those Afghan detainees needed to be helped. So, in this delicate situation, we needed to be very careful and tactful in order to avoid defamation on one side, and the loss of our people on the other. I immediately contacted people who had contacted the media to consult them. Consequently, we decided to keep the hostages for the moment and eventually release them in exchange for the release of the Taliban detainees.

WITH WHOM DID WE TALK ABOUT THE THREE FOREIGNERS?

After we decided that we should release the hostages, we immediately contacted the Taliban Minister of Intelligence, who was then with the government, on October 30, 2004 and told him that we wanted to release the hostages because there were women among them. We told him to take care of this issue as soon as possible. After some time, he told me that the government said they could free the hostages by force. We could not reach him after that. Although he ended his contact with me, I waited for two more days, but we heard nothing from him again. After that we contacted a person by the name of Ahmad Ratib, who was a relative of Hamid Karzai and an acquaintance of mine. He showed interest and told me he would get back to me after he investigated, and looked into how he could help. After three days, he assured me that this would happen; however, he would have to win the government's trust first. He added that once he was certain about everything, he would let us know. After some time, Ahmad Ratib sent a message that he wanted to meet me personally. He came to Quetta by plane and we had a meeting in the Kuchlak area to discuss the issue. The captors wanted to be paid for what they had spent on keeping the hostages, something that was understandable. Unfortunately, it is common in negotiations that expenditures are described as higher than they really are and that the parties then agree on something in the middle. I mentioned our detainees and gave him a list of prisoners that we wanted released. Ahmad Ratib did not respond negatively to hearing any of this. He took the list with him and said that he would go back to Kabul the next morning and let us know after he shared our suggestions with the officials there.

We waited for a while and apparently the government wanted to delay the deal. Ahmad Ratib said that after he returned to Kabul and shared what we had told him, officials in Kabul started investigating him instead of being happy about the deal, despite the fact that he'd had their approval prior to coming to Quetta. The investigation and questions focussed on how Ratib knew us, how long he had known us and where we were at the moment. I had the impression that these people wanted to deceive us, so I stopped everything I was doing at the time. It was possible there were people in contact with him who did not want this case to be resolved. After that I still tried calling him on his phone, but he would not answer. A few days later, Mullah Nuruddin Turabi, who was Minister of Justice during the Taliban rule, phoned me and told me that Mullah Malang wanted to help resolve this issue as soon as possible. I told him that Mullah Malang had done little to recommend himself. He once left the jihad for money and had since changed sides to the non-believers. Mullah Nuruddin Turabi insisted that I talk to him. Due to his insistence, I agreed to talk to him, but it was a mistake. How could someone who has not been loyal to his God be loyal to me?

I would like to give you a brief introduction to Mullah Malang. He was a mujahed by name alone during the jihad against the Russians. He was not known for fighting well against the

Russians, but for killing innocent and helpless people without any trial. There was even a well named after Mullah Malang, because he would throw people he had killed into it. Everyone in Kandahar knew this. At the end, as a result of torturing innocent people and betraying the holy jihad, Allah defamed him. I have personally witnessed some of his immoral actions and have heard about others. I went to Islamabad from Quetta to see Sayyed Abdul Karim Agha who was head of the Harakat-e-Inqilab Islami's Quetta office's military section. After greeting each other, I asked him about Mullah Malang; he told me that Mullah Malang was in jail for kidnapping somebody's wife. The woman's husband came and put him in jail. Mullah Malang eventually arranged his release for money. Not only this, but in the last days of the jihad, he abandoned and criticised it. He would say that he could not enjoy even spilling the blood of a bird. He then drunk alcohol and even denied that it was *haram*. He would say that alcohol produced from fermented pomegranates was *haram*, but not the alcohol produced by machines from chemical substances. He had several other vices that it is not necessary for me to mention here.
Our great mistake was that we did not act according to the saying of the Prophet (PBUH) that says that "A Muslim must not be bitten twice by a snake from the same whole". We were bitten by Mullah Malang several times in the past and we had tasted his poison, but we forgot. When he told me that he had loved me since the time of the jihad and that he hadn't changed, I let myself forget his ways and prepared to make the deal. I did everything out of the trust I had in Mullah Turabi, but it was possible that he did not know him well either, because he was a committed and honest mujahed.

I finally answered Malang's phone call; he kept saying that he was ready to help us in any way that he could, and that he was immediately going to go to Kabul to take care of the issue. I was in a hurry as well and wanted to be done with it as soon as possible. After his arrival in Kabul, he contacted me again. Meanwhile, many other people got ready to mediate on this issue, because unfortunately everybody wanted to get close to the non-believers and earn some money in the process. Mullah Nuruddin Turabi supported him, and told me that it would be good if we resolved this deal through Malang. Despite his betrayal, I promised that I would definitely do it through him, but that he needed to be quick in Kabul. I wanted to finish this soon and that is why we gave control to such a traitor. Malang was very pleased and started his work in Kabul. He contacted me via phone several times and spoke to me about the issue. After a while, he told me that he had taken care of things on his side, so he wanted us to discuss our proposals. I told him that I wanted 24 of our detainees and that the people who had had expenses wanted to be reimbursed. Mullah Malang agreed and after a while, he contacted us saying that we would be given the money before the release of our detainees. However, I was not happy with the release of the detainees coming later than the money. I knew what Mullah Malang intended: he wanted to take all the money for himself. So I backed out, but he insisted that I should trust him and he even said that he could offer his family in Islamabad as a guarantee. As I was thinking about the quick release of the hostages because there were women and children among them, and Mullah Nuruddin Turabi insisted that I trust him, I once again decided to trust him. At the end, we released those people because we trusted Nuruddin Turabi and were assured by him.

Meanwhile, there were still some people who wanted us to kill the hostages, so we had no choice but to agree to the deal. Mullah Malang assured the captors that he had the money and that they should tell their people to release the hostages. He claimed he would get the 24 detainees released once they were brought to one place, as they were in different provinces at the time, according to him. The captors understood his untrustworthiness and I was very worried about the detainees. Deals with such people never end well. Still, we made the deal because of our trust in Nuruddin Turabi and Walaswal Hakim. Mullah Malang was supposed to contact the government at the time of exchange to bring our detainees, but when he was given the hostages, he only contacted me and said that I had made him proud by doing the deal and that he would never forget what I did for him. He also told me that he would fulfil all the promises he had made. When I inquired about the detainees, he told me that I should not worry and that he would be able to get them released once they were all brought together at one location. After some time, he turned his phone off and on the rare occasions when he did answer, he would not give us any clear answers. A while after that I was arrested. I suspected him of being involved in my arrest, because he had contacted the captors and still promised that he would release the detainees. However, there were many other signs of his deception. For instance, he was once nominated by UNAMA to be a representative of the Badghis people, but he did not win as the people knew what a bad person he was. Another sign that he was two-faced was that he did not even ask about me when I was in custody. Not only that, he also opposed the efforts made to get me released. He asked some of those people why they wanted to release the second Mullah Omer. He would also encourage foreigners to go and talk to Karzai and other high ranking officials, asking them not to release me. Thankfully, Karzai expelled those foreigners who were Mullah Malang's friends for interfering in Afghanistan's internal affairs. That was when I became immune from his harm. Nobody else opposed my release, because most Afghans did not have any particular problem with me; only the foreigners wanted to keep me in detention longer, but Allah paved the ground for my release.

THE PAKISTANI THIEVES' TREATMENT OF ME AND THE OTHER DETAINEES

As soon as we arrived at the ISI office, I was taken to jail. The black bag was taken off my head at that point. The room they had put me in was made of wood. A man came into the room shortly to interrogate me, the sort of man whose cruelty was written on his face. First he asked me my name, the names of my father and mother, sisters, brother, wives, daughters and sons. I answered accordingly. After that, he asked about the time of the jihad, and I had no idea of the answers to many of his questions. I was treated terribly during the interrogation. You would think I'd been a Muslim captured by non-believers in a face-to-face war. There was no sign of Islamic behaviour in him, and sympathy and mercy were probably unknown concepts to him. I thought to myself that they should have named the country Faseqistan, the land of immoral people, instead of Pakistan. It was clear that they were happy about what was happening, because they doing good business selling the heads of Muslims to the Jews and non-believers. People of this region, and the entire world, know that these bulls will do anything for money; they would even sell Islam and their honour very happily. They had already made many deals for the heads of Afghan and Arab Muslims with Jews and non-believers. They even extradited a zealous Muslim woman, Aafia Siddiqui, to America. In addition, they handed over many other Arab Muslim women to non-believers for money and some other benefits. From my point of view, such people could not be considered Muslims and if anyone called such savages Muslims, his own faith would be questionable.

Whenever they decided to beat me and make me suffer, I would laugh at them. They did not beat me when they interrogated me on the first day; that was a Friday. They tied my hands from the back and put the black bag back on my head; then they took me to a very small room, which was about 1.5 m long and 0.75 m wide. The room had a very small window, which they closed. I could hear other prisoners, so I knew there were other people locked up there. I suspect they were also brought there just for being good Muslims, as they would recite the Qur'an and their voices would echo in the jail. When they took me to that room, I heard a voice from someone who I could not see saying that I should not worry as all these problems would pass and almighty Allah would help me get back to my home. Similar words were said, which calmed me, because that was my first time in such a jail cell.

As the time passed, I became familiar with everything and understood there were many other people like me there. Two days later, they took me somewhere else from the dark room. I could see other prisoners and could talk to them as well. Most of the inmates were clerics and Mullahs from Pakistan and Afghanistan. There were a small number of Arabs as well, who would always recite holy Qur'an passages and prayed. They would recite Duhayee Qonoot after morning prayer and when the guards were away, they would talk to us as well. When the guards came, the code among the prisoners was "We seek refuge in Allah from Satan the accursed one", to inform each other that a guard was coming and to stop talking. If the guards caught anybody talking to someone else, they would punish him badly. One day, one of the soldiers acted as if he was naïve and started asking me some questions very politely and in a kindly manner. I answered his questions with a broken heart, but he suddenly got mad at me, asking why I was not calling him “Sir”. I told him that I was not calling him “Sir”, because my “Sir” was only Allah and that I could not call a savage like him “Sir”. He warned me that he would see me in the evening. I waited, and thought he would come and torture me, but the night passed and nothing happened. I found out later that he was just an ordinary person who did not have any power.

On the first day, when I was taken to the jail, an officer came to my room and told me that he wanted to inform me of the rules that prisoners were bound by. First was not to talk to anybody and that if I was caught talking I should expect punishment. Second was to never raise my voice or scream. Third was that I needed to finish urinating and getting ablution in two minutes, and taking showers in five minutes. Also, I could not ask to go to the restroom more than once. I said OK. In short, everything there was contrary to human dignity and honour and aimed to disgrace us. For example, when a detainee would go to the restroom, he was required to leave the door ajar, so that except for the genitals, his body parts were seen while two guards were standing at the door calling on him to hurry up. They would use bad words. As our prophet and holy religion emphasises cleaning yourself after urination, I would do that, but the guards would get mad at me, curse me and sometimes even make fun of me, because that looked so strange to them. Anyway, there was no person of dignity among them and they were all trained to disgrace us. In the mornings, they would put us in light handcuffs and shackles, but in the evenings, they would put heavier ones on us which were very sharp and painful. The lighter handcuffs and shackles had ISI signs on them and were kind of loose. They would not give me much trouble. Still, they were handcuffs and shackles and may Allah protect all Muslims from them.

They would take me out and interrogate me every day. The interrogation room was close to my cell, but the black wolves would still put the black bag on my head just to make me suffer and humiliate me whenever they took me there. I had not given them my real name at first, so when they interrogated me on the second day, they wanted to determine my correct identification. A black general whose face showed no sign of being Muslim, and could easily have been a guard from hell itself, came close to me, clearly intending to beat me. He beat me, and on the third day they asked me the same questions, in addition to torturing me more. One of the generals asked questions, and another was responsible for torturing me, as the cruelty on his face suited torture.

On the fourth day, which was a Monday, they took me in for interrogation again. On that day, the interrogation was delayed and, as I had the black bag on my head, I couldn't see anyone, so I just sat and waited on the chair in the interrogation room. I suddenly heard somebody speaking. I heard chairs being arranged and people's footsteps. Things became silent and everybody seemed to have gotten in their place. They took the black bag off my head and I saw three Americans sitting there. Two of them were older and one was a young guy. The older men were relatively polite, but the young one was incredibly immoral. He told me that he would make me stand bare naked and use chemicals to remove all the hair on my body. The other two simply asked me questions and didn't do anything immoral.

Compared to the black-faced animals, the Americans were much less savage. Also, the black-faced Pakistani general did not do anything or say anything impolite in front of them. One thing the Americans insisted on was knowing my correct identity, and they warned me that they would hand me over to the northern alliance if I refused to give them my correct name. Back then, they thought that they would divide Afghanistan into two parts, the north and the south, to create tension and disputes, because their main plan was to divide Afghanistan further. Sometimes they would threaten to take me to Guantanámo.

They left that day and the black-faced Pakistani general came, wanting to beat me again, asking why I didn't cooperate with the Americans or even give them my real name. The black-faced Pakistani general was a thief as well, because when they raided my house he took a lot of equipment, cash, a watch that cost 120,000 Kaldar, three computers and some other items with him. He beat me every day for embarrassing him by not giving my real name to the Americans.

The Pakistanis regularly made deals for the lives of Muslim people. Due to their love of money they sold many Arab women

and Taliban. At other times during my detention, I came to understand that when it came to beating us, the non-believers showed much more humanity than the Pakistanis.
During the next day of interrogation, they kept insisting that I had to tell the truth and not upset their associates. However, I did nothing but laugh. My laughter was for two things: one was that they wanted me to help them; and the second was their pretence of friendship. The Americans left that day and the black-faced general beat me badly. My mouth was filled with blood, but he called other soldiers to beat me as well. Everybody beat me with whatever they had in their hands. Still, they did not beat me anywhere near as badly as the general. They had special equipment to torture the prisoners with. They had some flat pieces of wood that they would use to beat the prisoners' waists. They also had some sticks to beat us with. Finally, the general had me stand next to the wall broke two of my molar teeth, filling my mouth with blood. He still wanted me to give my real name to the Americans.

The ISI mole who had given them my information, and could have been one of my close friends, had given them a photo of my brother to help them. That photo gave them another excuse to beat me and torture me. They asked me if he was my brother, but I denied knowing him. After I was released, I asked my brother about that photo and who he had given it to. After thinking for a moment, he remembered who had had the photo. He also gave me some other information about him and we realised that he was a close friend of mine. May Allah guide everybody to the right path and make all of us true Muslims. God knows best about everything that happens.
I had claimed to be Hafez Abdul Karim from Arghestan, who was a great commander and was martyred during the jihad. My friends had created a Pakistani ID card for me under his name. My insistence made them come to the conclusion that they had the right person. It was amazing that journalists clearly helped them and revealed many secrets to them, because they told me about what they had learnt from journalists. The threats and abuse continued for some days, but stopped after that. After 27 or 28 days, they came again on a Friday; the black-faced Pakistani general told me that I should help them. I asked how; he said that I should give him the truth. I laughed, but it was

laughter from pain. I asked how he expected me to help him destroy me. Anyway, regardless of how much he insisted, I did not give him my true identity. During my stay there, I saw two areas. One was the place I was first brought to and the second was the underground rooms I was taken to later on. They had very humid air and were very frustrating. Some time later, they took me to another place that had eight rooms and after that they returned me to my original location. This place was slightly better as the inmates were mostly clerics and religious people. It was better ventilated as well.

Another torture method was to deprive the prisoners of sleep. The guard would come and knock on the door and the window every five minutes to prevent the prisoners from sleeping. Another torture was that a group of them would come at about 2:00 AM when everybody was asleep. They would ask the prisoners to stand facing the wall and not turn around. Then they would search our beards and head hair, and all over our bodies. When they came, they would spread horror when they knocked on our doors. They would go to all the cells and then leave. This was done every day and they never missed it. Nobody else could come to visit the detainees or bring them anything, and this was done just to torture the prisoners physically and psychologically. The food was very bad and most of the times they would bring left overs for our meals. Everybody could figure out that the food that was brought was left overs.

TAKING ME TO PENDAI

I spent 38 nights in the Karachi jail. On the 39th afternoon, they made me change clothes and then handcuffed me, put a black bag over my head and put me in a car. Although my face was covered, I felt that they were taking me straight to the airport. I was not sure of what they wanted to do with me and where they were going to transfer me to. It seemed that they wanted to hand me over to the Americans, because when I got on the plane, I heard English being spoken, so I became certain that they were foreigners, but then I noticed that the people who brought me from the jail were still with me. Then I suspected that they could be Pakistanis. I was thinking about this until we got close to Islamabad. At that point, I understood they were

Pakistanis. It was interesting that even though I was handcuffed, shackled and then tied to the chair on the plane, they still wanted me to pray for them as the plane took off. Although they were certain about the truth of Allah's religion, they accepted slavery. They had left Allah's path and chosen slavery. It was late afternoon and prayer time, so I asked for permission to pray, but they did not let me do so. I had to pray by pointing, as I was tied to the seat.

Finally, it was the evening when we arrived in Pendai airport. They put me in a vehicle and quickly took me to an ISI base. After that they took the handcuffs off my hands, but tied me with a big chain that had big thick links. Then they locked the chain to the windows. That detention centre had more facilities than the one in Karachi. The food was not bad either and there was no restriction on ablution or using the restroom. Also, there was no night time searching. I was kept there for almost six months. There were many other prisoners there and most of them were imprisoned for political reasons. I was always kept away from them, and could only go near them when I was getting ablution.

HANDOVER TO THE AMERICANS

It was around ten o'clock at night, and I was performing prayer, when the door of my room was opened. I was very concerned; after the prayer, two of the soldiers came into the room and took the handcuffs off and put new ones on. Then they covered my head with that black, awkward bag again. They took me out of the jail and put me in a vehicle. The destination was the airport again. I became sure that the black-faced dealers were going to sell me to non-believers and hand me over to the Americans. Upon our arrival at the airport, American vehicles came near us. They dragged me so roughly that you would think it was a wolf dragging a sheep. They took me to the nearby building by dragging me ruthlessly. There, they put me into a small vacant room and tore my clothes. Those cruel savages had me stand bare and left no cloth on my body. In this shameful condition, an American who had a goatee took pictures of me from all sides. I was very sad, but I am happy almighty Allah put me in the condition Abraham was put, as Nimrod had thrown him bare into a fire. Allah will reward him on doomsday. I believe Allah will reward me for all those hardships I went through, because he is just and merciful. After taking pictures, they gave me a thin shirt and trousers which were intentionally torn up to the knees. They pulled me up to the plane even though I showed no resistance to walking. They just wanted to torture me. When they got me on the plane, they tied my hands with some type of cord that would peel my skin if I moved my hands. Suddenly, they covered my ears and eyes with tape and then tied me to the chair. Allah helps a Muslim every moment; at the beginning, I was not very concerned, but when the savage Punjabis handed me over to the Americans, I became certain that they were going to take me to Guantánamo and made my mind up that I had nobody else left but Allah. I didn't even expect anything from my relatives. That mindset gave me some peace of mind. I started praying. The plane landed after an hour of flight. I did not know what airport that was, but I was just guessing it could be Bagram, where they might want to change the plane or refuel, because it was common that Americans would take prisoners to Bagram before they took them to Guantánamo. In fact, it was not Bagram at all.

HANDOVER TO AFGHANS AND THEIR TREATMENT OF ME

I was taken to court for my first trial without being given any of the legal rights I mentioned above. Before anything else, I should have had a defence attorney; I should have had the right to see the indictment and prepare my defence statement accordingly. The prosecutor should have sat with me and informed me of what I was charged with. I was given no legal rights.The judge was from the Shiite sect and would get mad at me, even though judges should not get angry and never have the right to insult the accused. The judge was already biased and told me that he was forced to conduct my trial, while judges should be independent in their decision making; he also had a prejudice based on his religious sect. He was very rude and treated me poorly during the trial. I asked for a defence attorney and he agreed, but he did not agree to let anybody visit me or instruct NDS officials to let my family members visit me, because I would be able to hire a defence attorney through them. When I was called for the second trial, the trial was once again not properly conducted. Then I was brought for the third trial and when I asked for a defence attorney for the third time, the judge cursed me and told me that if I did not hire a defence attorney in five days, he would have the trial in my absence. When I was taken to the detention centre, the clerk brought me a letter informing me of my sentence. They violated all of my legal rights. According to the letter, the court had sentenced me to 16 years' imprisonment.

Despite all those illegal actions and cruelty, I still relied on Allah and I was strong in my faith, believing that the only just being was almighty Allah. I believed in his decision. I did not get upset after reading the letter informing me of my sentence; I did not become worried either. I just felt sorry that there was not a single person in the whole system who my voice could reach about these unjust and illegal actions. As time passed, they let me have visitors; the first time, they brought me another pair of clothes and 500AFN. I was very happy to have the money, because I was able to get out in the sunshine after I gave the money to the soldiers. The Pakistani puppet government had arrested two other innocent Afghans by the names of Ustad Yasir and Hakimi and had handed them over to the Americans in a deal. A short time after they were brought here, they were permitted to go under the sun and I would just observe the situation from the window. I also asked the commander of the detention facility to let me go go out in the sun too; he accepted my demand and let me go out. After that, I was able to go out in the sun as long as I did not talk to anybody outside. I would talk to them anyway. One day an NDS employee told me that a high-ranking official would come and see me that day and that I should wait. I did not know who was going to visit me. That afternoon, a senior figure from within the NDS came. He greeted me warmly and treated me with respect when he talked to me. Before he left, he gave me 2,000 Afghanis and he also instructed the head of the detention facility to let me have visitors. He told me and Hakimi to come up with a list of things we needed so that they would provide them for us. We prepared a list hastily and he later sent all the items we had listed. The head of the NDS' 17th branch did not like the situation, and was infuriated. He had told somebody else that they could not have any deals there and that the detention facility was not anybody's personal property, to have whatever they desired. One would think he had inherited NDS from his father. He was extremely cruel, and was known as Naf Kash (Navel Remover), because he would bite the detainees' navels when he got angry. He had no real personality, and had deep linguistic and regional prejudices. The head of the detention facility was from Panjshir. He had taken $ 44,000 from my visitors and had claimed to represent the head of the NDS branch. When I found out, I told them all about what had happened. I don't know what took place between them, but apparently one was removed from the detention facility after a long dispute. After that the head of the NDS branch held a grudge against me. He beat me badly one night to the extent that he tore out one side of my beard. He was an immodest person, and cursed my father and mother. God knows that I was not as affected by the beating as I was saddened by his cursing words. It is common in Kandahar that zealous people won't curse while fighting regardless of how much they get hurt. He beat me under the pretext that I had contacted the Amir ul-Mu'mineen Mullah Mohammad Omar Mujahid via telephone. That night was full of trouble for me, and thanks to Allah everything in this world passes, no matter if that thing is grief, happiness, comfort or trouble.

The NDS branch head sent someone for me the next day and summoned me to his office. I thought he was not yet calm, so might torture me again. When I went there, I realised he had called me to apologise, just like a proverb that we have: "Sitting cross-legged after farting". He said that he was sick and under pressure and that that was why he had beaten me. I told him that I did not mind getting beaten and that I was in their custody, and they had the ability to treat me however they wanted, but that my father was a well-known cleric related to a religious family. Also, my mother was from a very well-respected family, so I was very much upset when he cursed them. He said in response that his father had been governor of Bamiyan province in the past. He was stupid to mention his father instead of apologising, when I had not cursed his father at all. His comparison seemed funny to me, because he compared thorns with flowers. Anyway, I was the oppressed there, and in his custody, so I could not discuss my opinions and I simply nodded as he talked. After he was finished, I went to my room. When the high-ranking NDS figure asked for my list of necessities, the section head was angry once again. He arbitrarily arranged a transfer, to punish me and get me away from the more senior figure so that he would not be able to help me and, he claimed, would not interfere in his personal affairs. He took me and a few of the other detainees to Pul-e Charkhi prison.

MY TRANSFER TO PUL-E CHARKHI PRISON

Pul-e Charkhi prison is well-known among all prisons and we had heard horrible stories about it, which scared us. Therefore we were concerned about our time there. After we arrived at Pul-e Charkhi and passed through the main gate, we were taken to the fourth block. He immediately introduced me to the commander of the block. He recommended that they arrange a separate place for us from other inmates. We spent the first day and night in a public room. In that one night, I figured out that ranging from the commander of the block to officers, soldiers and ordinary guards, they all did different things to inmates. The commander of the block came around late that afternoon and divided us into different groups. Hakimi, Mawlawi Asadullah and some other people were with me. They took me to one of the wings. I was very concerned as I was new there and did not know the situation well, but God does not upset his committed human beings. There were people who recognised me as a committed mujahed and respected me a lot. They gave me food, left the best spot for me and treated me well, generally. However, wings in the prison are places where thieves, adulterers, immoral people, bandits, drug addicts, Talibs, Mullahs and people of good personalities are all together. Any type of person could be found there. The TV was on during the day and night; some of them would listen to superstitious music. It was an unpleasant environment.

After a short while, the commander of the block came to see me and told me that he would take me to a safer part of the prison, because somebody had made some recommendations about me to him. So he thought it would be better to provide me with a good cell before somebody told him to. That's when I was taken to a smaller wing called "Earing" by the prisoners. It had a large space and had water and other necessities. By that time, the senior NDS official had become aware of my and some other detainees' transfer to Pul-e Charkhi and why that was done. So he had called the commander of Pul-e Charkhi and had told him to take care of me. Then the prison commander sent someone for me who took me to the commander's office. There he told me that the senior NDS figure wanted to talk to me and he then handed a phone to me. I grabbed the phone and started talking. He was well aware of the situation and asked what I needed him to do for me. I said I wanted a separate room where I could recite the holy Qur'an. He told the commander to give me whatever place I wanted. I just showed him a room that had a restroom and a study room. Commander Samir Khan immediately gave the room to me. Hakimi was a very patient and good person and he would memorise the holy Qur'an as well; I took him with me and went to the new place. That new place was comfortable compared to the NDS detention centre. Even though we had feared Pul-e Charkhi prison, almighty Allah gave us comfort there after so much trouble and hardship. God has said in his holy book (the Qur'an) that there is ease with hardship.

There is no doubt that Allah's and human beings' intentions are not the same. I was still happy at the NDS detention facility when compared to the Pakistani ISI jail. Meanwhile, I was more satisfied and comfortable in Pul-e Charkhi prison compared to the NDS detention facility. If one would think about great God's creatures and system, he would figure out that God has satisfied people who live in mountains with those mountains, desert inhabitants with the desert, city inhabitants with the cities, prisoners with the prison and then among prisoners he has made some happy with the fact that they have lesser time to serve. This satisfaction is not something that another human being could give to somebody or deny giving it to somebody else. One person could not control another person's heart. Because Allah blessed me I was able to memorise the whole Qur'an and made it my permanent companion while I was in prison. I was still serving my time in prison when the NDS section head was dismissed from his job and was replaced by Kamaluddin Gulalai, who was originally from Kandahar province. During the jihad, a minor dispute had taken place between us and Gulalai, so I thought he might have kept the hatred against us in his heart, because not only me but Taliban related fronts had disarmed

him. There were also rumours that the NDS overall chief, Amrullah Saleh, had some dispute with Kamaluddin Gulalai and that Amrullah Saleh was trying to bring the old section head for his own reasons. However, that did not happen and Gulalai stayed in that position. After much talk, we convinced Kamaluddin Gulalai to take the news of my innocence and the hardships that I had gone through to President Hamid Karzai. He took the beard hair his predecessor had torn out with him to prove to President Karzai that he was a ruthless person, especially when he treated such well-known figures this way. Gulalai became silent for a while and after some time they took me and the Taliban's spokesperson, Hakimi, who was a very spiritual person, to the NDS while his hands and legs were tied.
The fact that they brought us to the NDS separately made us concerned that something new could have happened. We did not have any choice but to wait; after a while, Gulalai came personally and after he greeted me, I realised he was in a good mood. He had a good chat with me and at the end he gave me a telephone to talk to my family. When it was time for him to leave, he asked how he could help me. I told him to tell the prison commander to leave our room door open so we could freely move around and go out in the sun. He agreed and gave us as much freedom as we desired. Kamaluddin Gulalai came again after a few days and asked if I wanted him to do anything else for me. I asked if he could allow us to have a telephone so that I could stay in contact with my family and relatives. He immediately gave me his phone and told me to ask my family to bring me my own phone. I contacted my brother and he brought me a phone the next day. Although having a phone while being in NDS detention was forbidden, he helped me a lot and what I had thought about him turned out to be completely wrong.

The Sadat tribe had good relations with the Achekzais in Kandahar and the surrounding areas. When Kamaluddin provided us with what we wanted, most NDS employees did not approve of it, because they were prejudiced and were from his predecessor's tribe. They started looking for ways to disrupt the situation, threaten us and send us back to Pul-e Charkhi prison. After some time, when Kamaluddin Gulalai had gone to Kandahar, Amirullah Khan came to the detention facility one afternoon, called the employees there and they decided together to transfer us to Pul-e Charkhi prison before it got dark that evening. Based on the law, detainees couldn't be taken from one place to another at that time because it was after official work hours. It had snowed a lot and the weather was very cold, but they had made up their minds to take us to Pul-e Charkhi prison. They told us to get ready to be taken to Pul-e Charkhi; however, we did not believe them as it did not seem to be the right time to transfer us. Regardless, a man came and instructed us to leave, as the vehicle was there to take us. Hakimi and I stood up and said that we wanted to perform late afternoon prayer, and that then we would go. However, they did not let us pray and told us that we could perform prayer on the way. When we got on our way, they did not let us perform prayer at all and we missed the prayer time. After we arrived at Pul-e Charkhi, we made up for the prayer when we performed the evening prayer.

SENT BACK TO PUL-E CHARKHI

It was the 15th of Jaddi when Amirullah Khan took advantage of the opportunity to send us to Pul-e Charkhi once again. Unlike the last time, they took us to the block where all the people incarcerated for criminal offences were kept. In that block, we were then taken to a wing where there was no mentioning of Allah or worship of Allah. I was sure that was happening to us as directed by Amirullah Khan, to put us with criminals instead of political detainees and thus punish us psychologically. They separated me and Hakimi; he was still taken to a better place compared to mine. When they were putting us into the block, the head of the block, who was a Laghmani, took my holy Qur'an from me. I told him that I needed it because I was memorising the holy Qur'an, but he replied angrily in foul language and took off my turban as well, even though I was allowed to wear my turban at the NDS prison. I reminded him of this, but he did not pay attention.

It was impossible for me to spend time there because kilos of narcotics would be brought there daily and would then be packed in smaller bags to be distributed round the entire prison. The employees were the contractors in this deal and were busy doing this all night. I asked them when they slept and they answered that they did from 3:00 in the morning up to 9:00 in the morning. Performing prayer, worshipping, humanity and normal human beings' daily affairs were unknown to them. Our room was so tiny that I could hardly sleep in it. They had told me to sleep under a bed where it was so tight that one could not move from side to another. There was a TV in that tiny room that always showed useless programmes, dance and immorality. The walls of the room were covered with naked pictures of foreign movie stars. In short, that place was incredibly sinful and living there was torture for me.

I would always say that "may Allah destroy him in both worlds," whoever had decided to punish me like that. Seeing the conditions, I decided to disregard the cold weather and go out to the hall, because I preferred cold weather to being in such sinful conditions. When I told my roommates that I was going to sleep in the hall, they told me I would be frozen and dead by the next morning. Then they sent me to another room where I could get along with the people. When we woke up at dawn, I called for prayer and three people came and performed prayer behind me. After the prayer, they told me that it had been three or four months since they had heard the call for prayer (*Azan*) and had not been able to pray in *Jumahat* (in a group) at all. They were happy that I was there; we started performing our prayers in *Jumahat* and the number of people praying grew from one day to another and finally there were 16 of us. Some people favoured religious studies, so I started teaching them; however, the people who did not have any religion did not like me. The political prisoners in blocks 3 and 4 got the information that Amirullah Khan had punished us, because Kamaluddin had treated us well. Amirullah Khan had great prejudices and had deep enmity with Pashtuns and Taliban. The inmates held demonstrations and one of their demands was to take us back from block 2 to our former location. Ustad Yasir had told the prison commander, Qais, that the demonstration could only be ended by Sayyed Mohammad Akbar Agha. Ustad Yasir came and both commanders came to our room. They promised they would take me back to my room, and they did. As soon as I got there, Commander Mohammad came and asked for my help to end the demonstration in block 3. I suggested that they should first hear the inmates' demands, so we listed their demands on paper and shared them with the people in charge. The prison officials at least admitted that the inmates' demands were legitimate and promised to ensure their rights as soon as possible. The demonstration was then ended and the problem was resolved.

THE INMATES' PROBLEMS WITH THE COURT, THE PRISON AND THE OTHER INMATES

Throughout my time in prison, and everywhere else, I came to the conclusion that it was not possible to pass time without money. A good example of this was the taking of nearly $50,000 from my friends by people at the NDS prison. I noticed that those of the inmates who had money had access to all resources. However, those who did not have money had the worst time. Similarly, if somebody spent some money while his case was under investigation, he would soon be out of the prison, but those who did not spend any money would serve months and years of in prison for even very minor cases. Political prisoners were very poor and did not have money and they would be satisfied even if they were being treated unjustly. For example, there were three friends in the prison and all three had the same cases. When their cases went to trial, one of them was sentenced to seven years, but the two others were sentenced to ten years of imprisonment, Why? When we asked, the one with lower sentence said that he gave the judge $ 1,000 when he greeted him and that is how he got three years less than his friends. Now, you can make your own judgment as to how you could have different sentences for the same crime and the same case.

Meanwhile, there were judges who were not corrupt and would not take money. They helped even the political prisoners. Nowadays, Afghanistan is in a situation where courts are not fully independent; foreigners interfere from one side and Afghanistan's NDS and other high-ranking officials get involved from the other side. A good example of this situation was my case, when the judge told me that he had been forced to issue a tough sentence for me; however, he did not tell me who he had been forced by and I did not understand whether that person was an Afghan or a foreigner. Also, before my release, Mullah Ma-

lang and foreigners tried to prevent my release, but fortunately those foreigners with whom Mullah Malang was trying to prevent my release were accused of interference in Afghanistan's internal affairs, and Karzai expelled them out of the country. I was released accidentally with the help of Allah.
Inmates in Pul-e Charkhi prison faced many problems and were generally in terrible economic circumstances. The prison was poorly equipped, the food was bad and there was no medication or doctors for when any of the inmates got sick. There was a clinic by name only, where they would give you the same type of pill regardless of what type of sickness one had. It is worth mentioning that 11 or 12 of the inmates at the block where I was died because of poisonous drugs and lack of doctors. Besides, prison employees had low salaries and probably had no option but to take money from inmates under one or another name. In other detention centres, they would let us have visitors twice or at least once a week, but in Pul-e Charkhi prison, they would only allow a visitor once every fifteen days.

There were tens of drug addicts in each block and the number was growing day by day. I want to tell an interesting story about this here: the commander of the block came and said that he wanted to separate the drug addicted inmates from the rest of them in order to cut the drugs from them and rescue them from this fatal problem. He said that the drug addicts' wing would be separate and the rest of the inmates would not be allowed to go there. They would be taking them out under the sun separately to prevent them from accessing the third block, because drugs were mostly distributed in the third block, where the officers would bring the drugs. Third and fourth blocks were adjacent to each other, so they could easily bring drugs there and then they would sell them at a very high price when the inmates of block 4 went outside. I and a few other people were very happy with the words of the Block Commander, and thought that those people might get past their drug addictions this way. As time passed, we found out that those inmates were separately brought under the sun and the rest of the inmates were not allowed to get close to them. However, we did not see any signs of recovery in them. One of the days I told one of those inmates that it was good that Allah had rescued him from his drug problem. He said that there was no rescue, but in fact they used to be able to buy a small bag for 50 AFN, but they now had to buy it for 100 AFN as the block commander had monopolised the drug supply. The commander was thinking about his own benefit and not the treatment of the drug addicts. We passed this news to other officials and eventually the block commander was transferred from that block.

ANOTHER SHORT STORY FROM MY PRISON MEMORIES

Whenever prisoners were brought to the third block from anywhere else, the officers and soldiers would not take them to the wings for about two hours. The new inmates would wait so that the guards could see what cases they had, or if there were relatives, friends or people they might know. Then they would divide them up and take them to different wings. They did this to find ways to get money out of the new inmates. Later on, if somebody wanted his friend to be transferred, or for himself to be transferred to where his friend was, the block commander or other officials would take money from them. One day I asked a representative of some of the inmates about how much money the block commander wanted to transfer one inmate from one place to another. He said that he wanted 200 Afghani and added that they also got about 100 mobile phones recently and then sold each of those phones two or three times through the canteen or other inmates for 2000 to 4000 Afghani. Better rooms were being sold and on the days they would allow visitors, meeting rooms were sold as well. Although it is the law that if any of the inmates gets sick, he should be taken for treatment outside and even abroad if needed, this was never the case there. Many sick inmates died. Very small numbers of inmates were released for incurable diseases. One thing that was mandatory in the prison was to give something to the block commander when an inmate's sentence was over. If an inmate didn't do that, the block commander would find an excuse to keep him there for longer. There was an incident once in block 3 when one of the inmates was due for release and the block officials asked him for shireeni or a bribe, but the inmate did not have anything. Then they had told him to get something from other inmates. The inmate had told them that nobody would give him anything, but that there was one inmate who used to be with him in NDS and was now in the 4th block and he might be able to ask him. They asked him who that inmate was. Then that inmate gave them my name; after that, I was informed that an inmate wanted to visit me and say goodbye to me. When he came, he told me that prison officials wanted money from him and he wanted to see if could help him, if not, they were going to delay his release. I gave him what I could afford. There was a lot of money in the narcotics business. One of the people who was involved in the drug business in prison said that he now had many cars, big houses and cash. I can't go into any more detail because there is so much more to talk about.

PROTESTS AND CASUALTIES

The inmates had a big protest in Pul-e Charkhi prison in 1388 (2009). Demonstrations had taken place before that as well. The main reason for the demonstration was that many inmates' cases were not being decided upon for years. One might have been acquitted, but the court procedure would not be complete; or you would see someone who was convicted by the primary court and would have served his sentence, but whose case was still pending with the appellate court. There were also cases where several people were held for the same case while only one of them had committed the crime. There were a great many problems in the system, and that is why the demonstration took place. Mediators helped a lot, and would listen to the inmates and then inform government officials of what needed to be done. With this mediation, the government promised to listen to the inmates and solve their problems, but did not fulfil its promises. In short, the government didn't care about the inmates' demonstrations at all.

In some instances, the lack of attention from the government caused violence during demonstrations, because there were all types of people in the prison. Political and criminal inmates were all mixed together and, contrary to what the law requires, inmates who were serving lengthy sentences were in the same place as those who were serving short sentences. The political inmates were mostly good people, because they were either Taliban, mujahedeen or clerics, who are respected people in society. The second group of good people were those accused of drug related offences, because they were in fact mostly business people brought there on false charges. In this environment, any protest would turn to violence, and almost every demonstration ended badly, because the inmates would not demonstrate legally, and the prison officials would not implement the law fairly and consistently. They had different rules for different people. They treated the inmates illegally and used the law as a tool for themselves, only implementing the law when it benefited them. However, if there was no benefit for them, they would break the law themselves.

If we look at prisoners' condition throughout the country, it is very saddening, because a variety of rules, laws, tortures and intimidation tactics are imposed on prisoners. Things that are happening in foreign forces' detention centres in Bagram, Kandahar, Shindand, Tora Bora and other locations are absolutely inhumane. How could you call torture and locking people in cages like animals the rule of law? I don't know if their law is like this. One of the people who was locked in Bagram prison and was later released came to my house and said that he was locked in a part of the prison called the Black Jail. They would give him food through a small hole; other than that he did not have any contact with the outside world and did not know prayer times at all. Guantánamo prison's devilish conditions have been put in words by Mr Zaeef and some other writers, so I will not mention those problems in detail here.

Meanwhile, some demonstrations took place due to very justified and reasonable concerns, but nobody wanted to act based on the law simple because the inmates were oppressed. During any demonstration, the prison officials would promise on behalf of the government that they would fully observe the inmates' rights. However, it was the same story of oppressed inmates, injustice and cruelty. From my point of view, the main problem with the prison officials was that they were mostly former communists and remnants of the puppet government. They wanted to dominate the inmates and impose any torture they desired. For example, visitors were allowed only once a week, while it is twice a week even in prisons run by foreigners or in other parts of the country. When the inmates protested in Pul-e Charkhi, the visitors schedule was changed to once every fifteen days. Sometimes they would ban visitors from bringing particular items. Political prisoners were not able to benefit from presidential decrees of forgiveness. The demonstrations finally became bloody. Another demonstration took place in Aqrab of 1388 (around October 2009); it did not look right to me from the beginning and I tried to stop it, because I knew the government would react violently and that it was about Eid ul-Adha time, when each of the inmates received new clothes and other gifts from their families. Some of the other inmates also wanted to stop the protest. I called those of the inmates who favoured the demonstration to my room and told them that I smelled blood from the demonstration and that I believed that it was not going to benefit the inmates. I knew that the demonstration was a lost cause and that nobody would care about them. In addition to telling them myself, I asked other clerics in the block such as Mawlawi Rohul Amin, Mawlawi Munir and Mawlawi Lal Mohammad to discourage those people from demonstrations. We gathered inmates' representatives from blocks 3 and 4 and told them that demonstrations did not have any benefit, but they were not convinced.

They finally agreed on a deal with the government. After the deal, block 3 officials attacked people on the block. The commander of block 3 was a former communist and still had a black heart. That's why he used weapons to attack unarmed inmates and killed more than twenty of them after making a hole in the wall of block 3. Nobody even asked about the people who were killed. Although governmental officials had agreed on a deal, they still attacked the oppressed inmates, including several clerics. Neither the block commander nor any soldiers or officers were prosecuted, or even replaced, for the gross violation of the law in that bloody incident. Instead, those in charge were commended. Inmates were being threatened and honourable people were taken to different blocks as a punishment. One of these, block 6, was also known as the 'drugs block'. It was the worst place; the rooms there were only 2×2 m with three inmates in them. Water pipes and toilets were in such bad condition that I cannot put it into words. Water would leak under the beds from the pipes and toilets. The condition was inhumane and far below Islamic standards.

The battalion commander wanted to do the same to block 4 as he had done to block 3, but the 'Guantánamo block' commander, Safiullah, and I prevented that from happening. I did this by contacting Commander Safiullah and telling him that block 4 inmates had not done anything illegal until that time and that they would not do so in the future either. However, if they wanted to get into a dispute with us and engage in violence, it would cause many casualties, which would ruin their reputation. After that, the commander quickly came and we discussed this issue. After that, they would take individuals from each block to punish them. My name had been on the list as well, but Commander Safiullah opposed this and told the rest of the officials that I had helped a lot and rescued the entire block from destruction. Also, defence Minister Abdul Rahim Wardak had instructed that they should not disturb me, so they left me alone. Bear in mind that ill treatment of prisoners was not something new in Afghanistan. During the Islamic Emirate of the Taliban, thousands of prisoners were martyred by the cruel General Abdul Malik in different ways, such as throwing them in wells, mass killings and torture. During the Taliban's time, the bones of oppressed prisoners who were martyred by savage Abdul Malik were brought out of those wells. Thousands of innocent people were buried alive; he used other horrible methods also, the mention of which would make your hair stand on end. The number of Taliban and local Pashtuns martyred as Taliban by General Malik is estimated to be about 100,000. That awful incident has not been matched in the recent history of Afghanistan and other countries in the region. It was unprecedented in its bloodshed and savagery. After the Americans attacked Afghanistan during the last moments of the Taliban's rule, another 12,000 Taliban who were stuck in the north, and surrendered to General Dostum, were martyred in one way or another.

From my point of view, the Taliban's leaders in the north made a big mistake by surrendering the Taliban to such a known cruel savage while there were many mujahedeen in the north. Although those mujahedeen had enmity with the Taliban, I am sure that if the Taliban leaders had talked to one of those jihad leaders and surrendered to them instead of to General Dostum, the Taliban would never have faced such a tragedy. Establishing contact with General Dostum and then surrendering that large number of Taliban to him was a plain mistake, and very unwise, because all those Taliban who were surrendered to him, along with Pashtuns in the north, were martyred by Dostum. Some others were kept in custody, but those who were kept in detention were in very poor conditions, because they were given very little food. One of those detainees who was eventually released for money told me about some of the problems in detention. He said that sometimes they were taken out to the prison yard to clean the yard where there were some type of bushes; they would collect the bushes and bring them to their rooms to relieve their hunger. Each of the detainees had a particular price; Pakistanis had one price and Afghans had another. Among Afghans, some were expensive and others were sold at different prices. That was when the Taliban's Islamic Emirate collapsed as a result of attacks by American and Coalition forces. At that time, many people related to the northern alliance were in Kandahar and many Taliban, and people related to them, were in Dostum's custody. The northern alliance got its people released with the mediation of Karzai from Kandahar prison; however, the Taliban who had survived the mass killings remained in custody. It would have made a good reputation for Karzai's government had it done what was promised.

Anyway, the inmates would be threatened in order to scare them off. The commander of the block was doing this to find ways of extorting money. He would tell an inmate that he deserved to be in block 6; the inmate would be scared and would offer to pay a large sum of money in order to prevent being transferred to that block.

MY SECOND TRIAL

My second trial was conducted illegally, as I had no lawyer, and the assigned prosecutor was not even present. Meanwhile, I was given only six days to present my documents. Despite this, the court sentenced me to 16 years' imprisonment, and broke their promise by sending the sentencing letter informing me of my sentence immediately after I was taken back to the detention centre. As I mentioned before, seeing the sentencing letter didn't make me sad, because I had faith in Allah...

When I called my relatives and friends while I was getting ready for the second trial, I told them that they should hire a lawyer for me so that he could work on my case and make my fate known. My friends told me that the president had promised that he would release me because I was a mujahedeen, and that they should not worry about me receiving a lengthy sentence. Still, I thought it was necessary to be careful and take care of this myself. My friends counted on the president's promise and did not try to hire a defence lawyer for me. So, I decided to hire a lawyer myself, one by the name of Mohammad Ibrahim Sahadat. Mr. Sahadat was both a legal expert and a mujahed himself. I had documents to present to the court, but they were not complete and were only later completed for the third trial. I was called upon to be ready for the trial. I was once again taken to court in handcuffs. The judge in my trial was a man named Dawood Bakhtiari, the chief Appellate Judge. The prosecutor was a Shiite with Communist sympathies, who did not treat me well. At the beginning of the trial, the prosecutor read the indictment. At the beginning of the indictment it was stated that I was a serious criminal. My first crime was being a mujahed who had fought and performed jihad against the invading Russians. The prosecutor had attributed other things to me that I was not aware of at all, much less had I done or seen them. I had not mentioned any of the things he was referring to in my statement, and none of them were in my file. Anyway, the prosecutor had invented these crimes himself and he had put them down on paper from his gut. According to the law the indictment should be based on the documents in the file. The prosecutor asked for the death penalty for me. What was amazing was that after twenty years of fighting against the puppet communists, at the end I was stuck in the hands of communists in a government that considered itself mujahed and anti-communist.

After the prosecutor finished reading the indictment, it was the turn of Mohammad Ibrahim Sahadat to read the defence statement. He did a great job and read a strong defence statement, starting by congratulating the prosecutor who considered the holy jihad, that was based on the fatwa of clerics from the entire Muslim world, and of which Afghans are proud, a crime. Similarly, he provided appropriate and convincing responses to all the baseless allegations made by the prosecutor. He effectively invalidated the prosecutor's indictment by pounding all the accusations with appropriate reasons and responses. Sahadat reasoned based on my file, and said that what the prosecu-

tor had said in the indictment was either not in the case file or was in contradiction with the case file.
The judge opened the case and read it carefully. He became sure that some things the prosecutor had put in the indictment were inaccurate and that the prosecutor didn't seem to be aware of the details of the case. You could tell that the prosecutor was nervous about my defence lawyer's presentation of the defence statement. The judge then pointed at me and asked what I wanted to say. I said that I did want to make some brief comments. After reciting "I seek refuge in Allah from Satan the cursed", and "in the name of Allah the most merciful and most compassionate", I recited a verse from the Qur'an where Prophet Yousuf is quoted saying, "I do not consider myself innocent, because one's ego directs him to vice." After that I added that my intention was not to compliment myself, but rather to prove my innocence. After that, I pointed to the prosecutor and started talking to him, even though it was the judge who had authority to make decisions about the case. I told him to either acquit me or punish me with long-term imprisonment. I asked for acquittal because at the time that I was being tried, an American by the name of Jonathan, who had set up a private detention centre where he would imprison innocent Afghans, was also arrested. Despite there being enough evidence against him, the Afghan justice system gave him a light sentence of ten years' imprisonment, and he was finally forgiven and released thanks to efforts made by the Americans. We were both arrested almost at the same time, but he was an American and I was an Afghan. He had committed an unforgivable crime and I had committed no crime. He was a non-believer and I was a Muslim, but still he was released and I was in custody. I told the judge that since it was clear they were punishing people based on their character, I would mention the character traits I possessed that were respected in Afghanistan. And, as with my recitation from the Qur'an, I was not complimenting myself, but I needed to mention these things about myself to prove my innocence.

First: My father, grandfather and other ancestors were all religious clerics, teachers and religious followers. They were respected members of society and were known to be honourable people by all my countrymen. The proof of this is that if anybody went to the Arghandab district and asked someone to show him Sahebanu's house, people would definitely show him our four or five families' houses, because the prophet's family is highly respected in our country, and related families are called Sayyeds, Sahebzadeh, MyaSaheb and other similar titles. Some people mistakenly call our village Naseran, while Naseran were actually our followers. Muqni Mahmood Saheb was a famous member of our family and his father, who was known as Khalifa Saheb, was our grandparents' Khalifa. Also, there are many clerics in our village; it is a sin to change your ancestry. There is a saying, "one who changes his ancestry in fact changes his religion".

Second: My second characteristic is that I am Sayyed, and from the children of the prophet. Sayyeds are respected by all Muslims, especially in our country, Afghanistan.

Third: Participating in holy jihad and my proud mujahed title was my third character trait. I became involved in jihad due to my commitment to my faith and Islamic belief when I was only a teenager. I joined the first mujahedeen front in Kandahar and I have not done anything other than jihad for my entire life. At that point, I showed the judge the scars on my body that were left from my injuries from the jihad, and told him that those were the signs of jihad. It is worth mentioning that there are three rewards for jihad, and the three are described in a verse of the holy Qur'an, "You may dislike something, but in fact that thing is for your good". For example, injuries on one's body are things that everybody dislikes and tries to avoid. The prophet's companions would use shields during wars. However, if one gets wounded during jihad, the reward from God becomes higher as there is a saying from the prophet, "On doomsday, that wound's blood would have the same blood colour but would smell like Mushk (perfume)."
Similarly there are many verses about the prosperity and good fortune of martyrs. They have been referred to as blessed, as God says, "Those who obeyed Allah and his prophet would be judged with those blessed such as prophets, honest people, martyrs and those with good deeds, and these would be the best friends for them". The third outcome of jihad is incarceration, because it is natural to dislike it, and human beings

are born free, so they like freedom. When they are locked up, they are fully removed from their nature, which is very difficult. Imprisonment is something that causes a real connection between a Muslim and his God, because during that time, only the assistance of Allah is important, and the love for other relations reduces. At that time, you don't have anyone else but Allah to ask for help from. As one is a *banda* of Allah and is in the custody of Allah at all times, one would become very obedient in such times. The above mentioned three things are in contradiction to human nature, and one's nature dislikes them and tries to stay away from those things, but they place you in good fortune with Allah.

Fourth: Knowledge is a quality for which Allah is well-known and it was for knowledge that Allah selected Hazrat Adam (PBUH) as his Caliph on the earth. It was for his knowledge that Allah selected Talut to be the leader of his nation. Allah says, "We increase his knowledge". And clerics are people who fear Allah because of the knowledge they have, as Allah has said that, "In fact, knowledgeable people fear Allah". That is because the clerics know all of Allah's power. Also, clerics have been referred to as inheritors. Thanks to Allah I am a cleric and have knowledge; I have spent most of my life teaching and studying. Religious studies and clerics are respected by the entire Muslim nation.

Fifth: Allah honoured me with memorising his word (the Qur'an) while in prison. Upon entering the prison, I decided not to get upset and to memorise the holy Qur'an. Although people find it more difficult to memorise anything as they age; I started memorising the Qur'an and asked Allah for talent and perseverance. At the end, I managed to memorise the entire word of Allah.

So I told the prosecutor to ask for five years of imprisonment for each of my qualities, which would make my entire sentence 25 years. I would just sit in Pul-e Charkhi and would not expect to be released. I would not ask anybody for help either. The judge and others present there were touched by what I said. However, the prosecutor called me a criminal, and wanted me to sit down and stop. I turned to the judge and asked him if they had called me there to be tried, or merely to hear the court's sentence. If the latter, then they could simply give me the sentencing letter and there was no need to waste anyone's time. The judge responded that I and the prosecutor had equal rights before the law; he said that I could say what I wanted to say. I then told the prosecutor that the head of the Investigation Department had called me about fifteen days ago and told me that I should ask my relative Amir Mohammad Agha to come, and they would release me provided that I live in Kabul. He told me that they would provide for my expenses and security guards as well. I told him that I did not want to incarcerate my whole family and that I preferred to be locked up by myself. The head of the Investigation Department did not like that and got upset.

I asked the prosecutor to go and find out why his boss wanted to release so-called criminals, and why he wanted to help them and provide their expenses and security guards. One could see signs of fear on the prosecutor's face upon hearing this. He got nervous and left the room without saying anything in response. The judge told me to go out of the courtroom and added that they would make a decision about my case. After I left the courtroom, the judge came after me and invited me to his office. He gave me tea and assured me that all evidence indicated that I would be released soon. I was waiting for the court's decision when the judge informed me that he was under pressure from some people and he could not make the right decision, so he had to either convict me to imprisonment or go to the Chief Justice and seek his guidance. Ultimately, he deducted two years from my sentence, leaving me with 14 years of imprisonment. It is worth mentioning that later I did find out who was forcing the judge.

MY THIRD TRIAL

When my case was referred to the third court (Supreme Court), I had completed all the evidence that I had presented incomplete to the primary and appellate courts. Meanwhile, the third trial was much more transparent and the judges were very good people, most of whom had been part of the jihad against the invading Russians as well. At that trial, there was no need for my defence lawyer and he was not asked to attend the trial, the decision was in fact made based on the evidence. I was sentenced to 16 years imprisonment in the primary court while I did not have a lawyer, and was not given a chance to provide evidence. In the appellate court, I mentioned how the judge made his decision under pressure from war lords and only reduced the sentence by two years. At the Supreme Court, the judge believed that I should be acquitted, because I was a famous person and led a party that had declared jihad against the presence of foreign forces in the country. That's why they had illegally imprisoned me for five years. Since I had already completed five years in prison, they decided to sentence me to eight years of imprisonment in order to protect the judges in my previous courts as well. Eventually I was released thanks to a presidential decree and due to serious sickness after five years and two months of imprisonment. Of this time, I spent a month and 14 days in the Pakistanis' custody, which was the worst part of my detention, but Allah made it pass; I spent over a year in Afghanistan's NDS detention and the rest of my time in Pul-e Charkhi prison.

I can say that there were definitely differences between Afghan and Pakistani detention facility officials. Pakistani officials treated detainees very harshly and used very humiliating words. The detainee would not know anything about his family and friends. Red Cross employees were not allowed to either give information to the detainees or transfer their messages. Much less were detainees, especially Afghans, viewed as human beings. In short, there was no observation of Islam and most people said that Pakistani detention was worse than Guantánamo. That was probably correct, because when the Americans came to interrogate me, they did not treat me as badly as the black-faced Punjabi general had. He would not beat us in front of the Americans, but when they were gone, he would start beating me. However, the Americans never beat me, although one of them with a beard was very rude. The Afghan government treated me better than the black-faced Punjabis. They didn't insult the detainees, and would let families and friends ask about detainees and bring in necessary items. The Red Cross would also be allowed to ask about detainees from time to time and would deliver letters from detainees to their families. Also, detainees were given warm clothes, thick blankets and some food during the winter.

THE WORK I DID DURING THE JIHAD AND TALIBAN TIME

During the first stages of jihad, when ranks and high positions did not matter, they would refer to me whenever a decision was being made about an appointment. However, I did not care for that area. At that time, the mujahedeen were short on weapons, and having weapons was of great importance. I was assigned to be the person in charge of weapon distribution and keeping track of them. Mullah Naqibullah Akhund, who later became one of the famous Kandahar mujahedeen, was assigned as my assistant. However, I did not care about the position and did not like ranks and high positions. I had a lot of influence in our front and I could get anything I wanted. Lala Malang got upset several times and I would bring him back without seeking the permission of the Mawlawi Agha, who was head of the front. The last time that he had gotten upset and I went after him to reconcile things, he made me promise that I and the rest of the Taliban would leave that front and accompany him if Mawlawi Agha made him upset again; I accepted what he said.

During that time, a large force came to our location and due to the injuries and martyrdom of many mujahedeen, many problems arose among the front, and caused disagreements between Lala Malang and Mawlawi Agha as well. The different beliefs of the two of them finally resulted in separation and, as I had promised Lala Malang, I decided to accompany him, although Mawlawi Agha did not think that I would go too. He sent a car after me, but I did not go with them. The health of the mujahedeen who were wounded in the war was more important than anything else; I rented a car and moved towards Pakistan to treat them. In addition to treating the wounded mujahedeen there, we officially got approval to open a front with the Islamic Party of Mawlawi Mohammad Yunis Khalis. At the beginning, I remained the deputy of Lala Malang at the office, and at the front as well, but after two or three months he was arrested by the puppet government, and I took charge of the entire front. Lala Malang was released after about two and half years, but was martyred a short time after that, so I remained the head of the front until the end. At the beginning, our fronts and military operations were focussed in the western region and when the councils were established, I would lead operations. Mujahedeen councils consisted of several jihadi fronts. Items donated through Pakistan would be given to the council leadership and it was necessary that the leader led the military operations of that front as well. I was the servant of the council, or in common terminology, the head of the council. Mullah Agha Saheb, who had Mullah Dadullah and later became an important military commander of the Taliban Islamic Emirate; and Mullah Mohammad Sadiq Akhund, from whose front Mullah Obaidullah later became Minister of Defence of the Islamic Emirate, were with us in the council. My brother, Mullah Abdul Salam Zaeef, was my partner in most stages of jihad. Another member of the council and jihadi operations was Amir ul-Mu'mineen Mullah Mohammad Omer Mujahed, whose friend Mullah Brother Akhund would also join us frequently. Haji Hayatullah Wardak; Mullah Shireen Akhund, who was a well-known mujahed with good management and knowledge, and had people like Mawlawi Abdul Hanan, Mullah Abdul Haq and other famous people who were well-known during the Islamic Emirate of Taliban, were with us too. It is worth mentioning that we never discriminated between mujahedeen of our front and other fronts, regardless of their membership in the council, they were always treated equally.

During the Taliban rule, when I came to Kabul temporarily and wanted to return, Mullah Nuruddin Turabi, who was Minister of Justice and head of the Complaints Hearing along with the Minister of Defence, Mullah Obaidullah Akhund, made me take responsibility for the first line front in Maidan Shahr. Since they were my friends from the jihad, I could not turn them away, so I assumed responsibility for the Maidan Shahr front for eleven months. It is worth mentioning that we had divided the first line in five significant areas: Jalrez, Nerkh, Jalga, Jaghatu and Chak. After that, I went back home.

During the American invasion of Afghanistan, I was busy with the affairs of my party, Jaish ul-Muslimeen. However, working on Jaish ul-Muslimeen was not because of any dispute with the Taliban, because disputes originate from difference in beliefs, while we had the same beliefs as the Taliban. We were no different to the Taliban.

MIRACLES OF THE MUJAHEDEEN DURING JIHAD

During the first days and nights of the jihad, mujahedeen were very committed to great God and had only good intentions. Nobody thought about position, power and wealth, so it was an obvious truth that divine light would be seen on many martyrs' graves, and when one would get close to the grave, there would be nothing there. Secondly, most martyrs naturally smelled very good, without using any perfume. This was a good smell that was different from any other smell in this world. I have personally smelled that smell, and it soothes human beings. Also, it was a miracle that the bodies of most martyrs would stay untouched in their graves, and their bodies were undisturbed despite several injuries, because most of the mujahedeen were far from their homes and according to shari'a law they had to be buried wherever they were martyred. According to shari'a law, it is respectful to the dead to take not take the body to another location. Sometimes, when relatives of a martyr would come and insist to take their martyr to their home, they would go and exhume the martyr; we would notice that despite the passing of a long time, the martyr was still laying sound in the grave.

Also, we can point out victories of small numbers of mujahedeen against large numbers of the armed forces of the red invaders as miracles of the mujahedeen, similar to the Badr fighters and Talut people, because the mujahedeen fought against a super power equipped with various types of weapons, artillery, tanks, war planes and helicopters, with only very old weapons, and few of them. Still, the mujahedeen would succeed as the Badr fighters did and as Talut's small group of fighters defeated a big army of Jalut with the power of almighty Allah. The holy war of the Afghan mujahedeen was the proof of this verse of holy Qur'an: "A small group would succeed against a large group with the order of Allah, and Allah is with those who are patient". Also during the jihad, there was an abundance of everything. All the deserts that used to be dry were filled with water, and older people said they had never seen that before. That was the bliss and miracle of jihad and the mujahedeen. The dreams of any mujahedeen in custody would mostly become true, because they would sleep according to shari'a. The messenger of God (PBUH) has said about this that revelation has ended now and after him it would be in the form of *mobashirat*. One of his companions asked the prophet what *mobashirat* was, and he replied that *mobashirat* was the delivery of good news through dreams. That is how the dreams of every detainee would become true.

Another miracle of the jihad and mujahedeen was that mujahedeen's prayers would be heard quickly. It happened several times that if somebody treated a virtuous mujahed badly, that person would get in trouble one way of the other. That was the time when mujahedeen were under severe pressure everywhere. Most soldiers were trained to treat detainees equally badly regardless of their innocence or guilt, goodness or badness, age, reason for detention, knowledge or lack of knowledge. One day a soldier told me that if he argued with a detainee and the detainee was killed in the dispute, it would not be a problem, but that if he got killed, he would be a martyr. He asked me if that was true, but I said that he would not be a martyr, but merely a cruel person. I told him that he could see what type of people the detainees were. Most of the political detainees were clerics, people who had memorised the Qur'an and people who were readers of Allah's words (the Qur'an). I told him that he could see how religious they were, because they would be busy performing prayer, reciting and memorising the Qur'an. Also, there was a madrassa where religious teaching and studying took place. Most of the detainees would fast outside of Ramadan month as well and would perform *tahajud* prayer. I should mention that most of the detainees would somehow get released before completion of their sentence. That was only as a result of prayers and virtue. There were even detainees would not be happy upon their release, because they would not have the opportunity to pray and worship as much as they could in the prison.

A SHORT SPEECH

I was given a separate room in Pul-e Charkhi prison because they recognised me as a famous person. During my last days, I would have somebody else in the room with me to avoid loneliness and somehow serve that person as well. I had invited a former mujahed, Dr Khaliqdad Akhundzadeh to my room. He was a very religious person and a brave mujahed. I knew him from the past and I was happy to have him there. We would both wake up for *tahajud* prayer. I would first wake up and perform some prayer by myself and would then call on Akhundzadeh. He would wake up, get ablution and we would then perform prayer in *jumahat* (together). We would recite the holy Qur'an until the morning prayer time. We would sleep for a short time after the sunrise. During the day, we would sit together, chat and talk about some religious issues. I told Akhundzadeh that Allah has said in the Qur'an: "I have not created the human beings and jinn for anything else other than worshipping". Prison is really a place for getting deeper recognition of Allah, thinking about him, worshipping him and returning to him. Allah has also said in the holy Qur'an: "Your wealth and children are seditions".

Before the holy month of Ramadan, a presidential decree of forgiveness that could include 22 people was issued. It crossed my mind that it would be a pity if my name was on the list, because Ramadan was coming and it would be a great time to worship. The entire holy Qur'an would be read in *taraweeh* prayer. In addition, I had memorised the whole Qur'an, but it was necessary to repeat that and Ramadan would be the perfect time to do that. That's what happened and I remained in the prison and spent Ramadan there. That was the only month of my imprisonment that I was happy. We read the entire holy Qur'an over and over several times. I would recite the Qur'an in *taraweeh* prayer and then recite it all night as well. It was amazing that my forgiveness order was returned from the gate of prison just as I hoped. One evening, the prison commander came to me and said how unlucky I was, because a forgiveness decree had come for me, but was returned from the gate. I was not upset about that at all and believed in the help of Allah. It was thanks to my reliance on Allah that another decree was issued three months later. My name was included in that one and I was released.
With the power of Allah, I was content in the prison and everyone stayed content with whatever prison time they had to serve. One would further return to Allah and strengthen his belief in power and the kingdom of Allah. There, one would know who really is in control of things: one who has some power in this world and rules tyrannically; or the God who is ruling over

hearts, who has created the earth and skies, and has created human beings as the best creatures as proof of his power. Allah is always alive and never dies and is owner of Judgement day. He is such a king that none of the kings on this world could reach even a fraction of his goodness. He is absolutely in control and that is good only with him, because he is very kind, merciful and just. You can see what varied human beings Allah has created and how he has given each of them different behaviours and characters. He has made some people happy with being nomads, some others with being residents, some with being in deserts, some with being in cities, some are happy with being in mountains and others in flat areas. He has soothed everybody's heart with what he has given them. He has even kept those in prisons satisfied despite being away from home, family and friends. If we look at it deeply, we understand that prayer to Allah would be accepted more quickly while being in detention, because that is when one is in very submissive condition. Allah fulfils desires of any oppressed person even if he is non-Muslim; however, Allah would fulfil a Muslim's desire more quickly.

THE COMPLAINT OF MUSLIMS ABOUT THE CURRENT GOVERNMENT OF AFGHANISTAN

It is obvious that the 30-year war in the country, the millions of casualties and the generally awful situation, especially the current situation, is the result of the Saur revolution imposed on the poor Afghan nation. The fire the communists lit up at that time has not died out after thirty years. After the establishment of the mujahedeen government, mujahedeen declared public forgiveness to all the remnants of the puppet government based on brotherhood, the desire for peace and their Islamic feelings. Although many mujahedeen were upset about that announcement and believed that there should have been prosecutions in order to punish those who had acted against the country and the people and sold them to the savage Russians, and acquit those who had not done so. Having done so, they believed we would have fulfilled the wishes of our martyrs, but that's not what happened. Mr. Mojaddedi seemed very happy while in power and wanted to remain in power, so he declared public forgiveness. He even went further and honoured some of the prominent communists by giving them ranks of general and giving them titles saying that they were 'Great Mujaheds'. I told him that it's unfortunate that he did not honour any of the mujahedeen with the rank of general, titles of 'Great Mujaheds' and other similar honorary titles, but instead he honoured the enemies of the mujahedeen, against whom they had fought for years. Do you consider this justice? Isn't the reason for all those things the fact that Mr. Mojaddedi was dreaming of staying in power for longer? He wanted to recruit supporters by making those announcements. However, that's not what happened, and much grief came to the country during that time, and after that as well. That was how remnants of the puppet government, and criminals whose hands were contaminated with the blood of innocent people, remained in the new government without being asked about anything.

After the invasion by America and its allies and the establishment of Karzai's so-called democratic government, those remnants once again got in power. Many important and key positions are controlled by them and they have full power. The government has given them the entire administration. They are in full control of the detention centres and prisons. Many good mujahedeen are spending time in prisons under their control. All the ministries are full of them; whatever they were doing during their reign, they do it now as well and even with a more open hand and lack of concern for the consequences of their actions. Meanwhile, the best thing for them is that whatever they do affects the reputation of the current government and nobody even mentions their names. They want to create an atmosphere where people will forget about their past cruelties and savageries, to the point that the public would believe that the communists' time was better the current rule.

Also, the foreigners are not here to build up our country and they never like to build us up or help us stand on our own feet. These are the people who spent so much money to collapse the communist regime. The communist regime collapsed as a result of their countless expenditure and many Afghans' sacrifices. However, the remnants of that puppet government now have power in all parts of this government without being asked about their past actions. If the foreigners' purpose really was to build Afghanistan, they would think about the past actions of the remnants of the communists. It is obvious that foreigners are using them to reach their own strategic goals here. They never care about Afghans' grief and destruction. Therefore, it is necessary for the real Afghans in the government to look back at their past fights and the actions of the communists and build their country independently in order to repair their homeland.

A LACK OF ORDER IN THE PRISON

It is a common practice in prisons all over the world to put inmates in separate rooms based on their age, type of crime and its intensity and and the length of the sentence, because mixing all of them would be disadvantageous for them and and the future of the society as well. However, this common and universal rule is not being implemented in Afghanistan. They had put inmates of different ages and crimes, such as murder, adultery, theft and more, all in the same block. It was particularly surprising that about 200 inmates were put in one wing. You would see inmates who were reading the Qur'an and memorising it while some others would be watching TV and listening to music. You would see some inmates gambling; in another corner, you would see inmates performing prayer in *jumahat*. Some would be asleep, because there was no set time to sleep. It was a place with many things happening that would make your hair stand on end. There were also many inmates who would listen to the clerics and would not continue with their past immoral actions. They would start studying religious subjects and turn to worshipping Allah. The prison officials did not observe the laws and did not respect elders, clerics and great personalities, as required by Islam and human nature. They treated all the good people the same way that they would treat the criminals, thieves and gamblers.

DEMOCRACY AND AFGHANISTAN

The word 'democracy' comes from Greek and, as with many other Greek words, it is comprised of two parts, 'demo' and 'cracy'. 'Demo' means people and 'cracy' means governing, so 'democracy' means the government of the people. Some people believe that the word 'democracy' originated from 'carsademos', in which 'carsa' means power/force, and 'demos' means the public. The entire word would mean the power of the public. Anyway, democratic systems consist of the people. In democratic governments, the government cannot do anything without approval of the public. The people can change the government via elections whenever they want to. In such governments, all high-ranking officials are selected by the people and the constitution of the country is also approved by the people. Every high-ranking official and the people in charge are held accountable about their achievements and actions. They are also held accountable for how they spend *bait ul-mal* (governmental funds) for the benefit of the public.

In general, there are three types of systems in the world: the first one is the royal system, in which all the power is with the king. Royal systems also have two types: relative royal and absolute royal systems. In relative royal systems, the king has limited power and parliament has the rest of the power; however, in absolute royal systems, the king has full power and the kingdom is inherited by the royal family. The second type of system is democratic. Democratic systems are divided in two types as well. In one type, the power is with the President and the two houses of the parliament, and if the parliament wants, they can impeach or remove the Prime Minister or any other minister. In the second type of democratic system, everything in the country is ruled by the President. The third type of system is Islamic Emirate. In this type of system, everything in the government is controlled by an Amir based on Islamic standards, an example of which was the Taliban Islamic Emirate in Afghanistan. However, the most transparent ruling was the ruling of the Prophet (PBUH) and after him the ruling by the four Caliphs. At that time, the entire Muslim nation was being ruled by the Islamic Caliph. Many countries in the east and west were under a united Islamic Emirate System.
I want to mention a few things about the royal system. Naturally, Muslims would like to spend their whole life under Islamic instructions and be submissive to God. They would like to choose justice, fairness and prophet-like behaviour, the principles of Islamic government. They should not forget Allah when they get in power. If they make good decisions, good for them, but if they get influenced by Satan and implement their own desire, they would have chosen the path of vice, just as stated in this

verse of the holy Qur'an: "I am not considering myself innocent and a person's desire direct him to vice unless Allah blesses someone. Allah in fact is the most merciful and the most compassionate". Therefore, virtue, fairness and justice, that Islamic governments require, have been forgotten, and tyranny has taken their place. The government has taken hereditary form; merit has been changed to lack of merit and those people who were capable of doing anything were killed or sent to jail. Some others were forced to flee from the country or they would have to suffer humiliation if they stayed in the country. History has witnessed that power has dishonoured respected people; thousands of people have been killed and thousands more have been forced to leave their country. In such conditions, the ruling person would keep people away from knowledge in order to prevent the rise of capable and talented people from among the public so that he would be able to continue his cruelty. Such a ruler would put bad people in power who would obey him, because if he put some talented people in positions of power, that would jeopardise his own position. That is why this ruler would not like talented people with merit inside their country, much less would he put them in any position of power. He would plot against such people to make them leave the country. In such conditions, the public becomes deprived both of religion and the world as well. Travelling abroad, education and doing business have become so complicated that most citizens cannot travel. There is one good point about the royal system: murder, kidnapping and fights take place very rarely. So, the people look at outward appearances and think that the King is just; however, he would have enacted strict laws to maintain his power. Members of the parliament are selected in a way that would listen to the King and consider whatever he says law and shari'a. They would keep them in ignorance of Allah's path. We have examples of past kings, like the Pharaohs and others, who kept their nations in the dark and deprivation, and the public would accept whatever the King said. That's when they would pose themselves as God to the public and the public would still accept it and obey them.

The second system is democratic, and that cannot be fair, just and based on human rights either, because parliamentarians get votes from people without being bound by any requirements and it is impossible that they would work for Allah's religion this way, because we see that everybody who votes asks for something in exchange for the vote; nobody votes for God's sake alone, and if somebody did, they would be in the minority. The parliamentarian has to fulfil the demands of the people who voted for him regardless of how legitimate or illegitimate those demands are. So the parliamentarians would have to do this in order to win the support of those people in the next election. Meanwhile, people in most of the world do not want the Islamic Systems in Muslim countries, where everything would be done according to Islamic standards. For example, I would mention Algeria or Turkey in the past when Muslims won the elections; the colonisers did not give them power and tried to return the power to the old rulers, because they did not want an Islamic government. It is a known reality that the Islamic system is based on fairness and justice, and human rights could not be ensured without implementation of celestial religion; democratic governments are founded on atheism . Democratic governments are formed based on who is the majority; there is no place for religion, because people with any religion, regardless of whether it was good or bad, would be able to write and publish news in order to put a spotlight on their religion and prove it true.

Third is the Islamic System or Islamic Emirate, which is founded on Allah's instructions. The public obeys the orders of Allah and his messenger in all affairs. The government implements the laws; the constitution is Allah's instructions. The people in power seek ways that would not contradict the instructions of Allah and his messenger, but would satisfy them. An example of this is the ruling of the Caliphs. Instructions are in the Qur'an and the traditions of the prophet. There are principles in the Islamic system. The first is honesty and the second is fairness and justice, as Allah has mentioned: "Your God's word ended with honesty and justice". Meanwhile, there is voting in the Islamic system as well, but through people of merit and commitment.

WHAT KIND OF GOVERNMENT DO WE CURRENTLY HAVE IN AFGHANISTAN?

If we think about the above discussion, we would notice that unfortunately destructive and fatal disputes have been going on in Afghanistan for tens of years. Enmity and hatred have been spread among families from house to house. This is still going on and is getting worse day by day. The so-called democracy that they talk about is not in place either, because democracy is a government that people like. In fact, this is a government ruled by power; anybody with power can do anything he want; he could be in control even if he had ruined this nation in the past and even if the public hated hearing his name and wanted to throw up upon seeing him. The rule of the powerful is still in place, and people do not have any role and are wasted and devastated every day. They leave the country or are arrested by one of the parties. Those who are arrested are not treated based on democratic principles; they are beaten up, tortured and dishonoured. I will discuss an example of this. From the beginning of 1390 (2011), we had been receiving complaints about one government organisation. The complaints were that many honourable people were being tortured at this organisation. Our information showed that the mentioned organisation would obtain confessions by force and then those innocent people were getting sentenced to lengthy imprisonment based on those confessions obtained through duress. After assuring myself and collecting reliable evidence, a few of us including Mawlawi Abdul Salam Zaeef; Mawlawi Wakil Ahmad Mutawakil; Raees Mullah Abdul Wahid Baghrani; Mullah Mujahid; Mawlawi Abdul Razaq, the Minister of Commerce; Mawlawi Nur Jalal, the Deputy Minister of Interiors and I went to see Mr. Karzai on the 20th of Jawza (July 10, 2011). The head of that organisation was also present, and presented some excuses that could have been due to negligence or lack of power. These responses were not convincing.

Also, American prisons and detentions centres are far removed from democratic principles. Dishonouring is widespread and I have heard about it personally from five detainees who were brought to my house by the prison commander. They complained that they had a place called the Black Jail where in addition to being tortured, they would not know prayer times and the guards refused to tell them. Food was put in a small bag and thrown through a hole. A few of the opposition leaders from the north criticised the government extensively regarding freedom of speech. Those talks were not for the nation nor were they honest. Many of the people in the public did not like their comments, but did not tell them anything. There is no democracy and the existence of an Islamic system could not be expected at all, because the Islamic system implements Allah's instructions and ensures humans' legitimate rights. It cuts the hands off thieves, executes murderers and stones or lashes adulterers. *Huduud* implementation is necessary; however, we don't see any signs of them in Afghanistan, because it contradicts the so-called democracy. The rule of the powerful is such a system, or disease, that neither respects Islam nor implements democracy, because they would like to do whatever is good for their own benefit regardless of its contradiction with Islam and democracy. In this system, there is more space for one's own wishes and everything is done based on desire. The royal system is not very common now, because it has gotten old. After all, the actions of the current Afghan government do not comply with any of the three mentioned government systems, so it has turned to a puzzle. A new nameless system is in place, because disputes have been going on for so long in Afghanistan. There has not been a government under which all people could gather and live in comfort.

DIFFERENCES BETWEEN THE TWO INVADERS IN AFGHANISTAN

Afghans spent the last few decades of life under systems that put them under psychological tyranny. They kept Afghans away from knowledge and culture and they left them behind in contemporary and religious studies as well. Political affairs were only up to the king and involvement by anybody was considered a crime. If an ordinary Afghan citizen would interfere in some political affairs, he would be considered a serious criminal and threat to the country, because that is how the absolute royal system works and even if there is security, it's for the King's own safety and ability to continue his kingdom. The public was neglected in a manner such that they would accept anything the King did or demanded. Little attention was paid to knowledge and culture in order to prevent the growth of talented people in the country who could become an obstacle to the King or his future heirs.

They would rely on other big countries and would ask them for everything. That is how the Russians took advantage of the opportunity and started long term movements in the country. An ill-minded party, the communist party, was established, and as time passed, they made that party dominant. There were Afghans who warmly welcomed the Russian control; however, it was still unwise for Russians, because Afghans were strict in their belief and faith even despite the prevalence of illiteracy among them. The Russians invaded the Afghans' religion; the communist regime, which is based on atheism, was expanded quickly and they wanted to impose rules other than Islam here on Afghans. They engaged in things like distribution of lands, equality of men and women and other similar things. However, Afghans' Islamic pride refused to accept this and did not let them implement their corrupted law in our homeland, although they used different tricks for implementation of their corrupted rules. They also made some failed efforts, such as creating committees most members of which were corrupted and immoral people. Each committee had a head and their duty was to put the public in hardship by any possible means. Another failed effort was to eliminate influential and famous people from the country. Many people are still missing and nobody knows what happened to them.

That was the only achievement of the past governments in Afghanistan: to keep the public ignorant and away from education. The lack of education and ignorance provided the Russians with a good opportunity to invade Afghanistan. They first put the communist regime in power and then sent hundreds of thousands of soldiers to Afghanistan starting various types of cruelty there. Millions of poor Afghans left the country because of them and emigrated to foreign countries. Many people were martyred and wounded. Tens of thousands of Afghans were disabled and lost their body parts. Russians would send forces to villages and would savagely kill any human or animal that appeared in their sights with a spray from an AK-47. In many villages, humans and animals would all be killed together to spread horror and fear among the public. They would send thousands of military vehicles, tanks, artillery and other military equipment to places where mujahedeen were and would stay there for several nights killing the people and destroying the villages. Russians would stay in face to face fights, but Afghans would also fight them back bravely. The Russians treated the people poorly and if one ran into Russians, all he could wish was that Allah rescued him. Executions of Muslims had become very common, especially; the domestic communists relieved themselves by killing Muslims.

Americans were thought of as believers in the past, but they were not any more, because they held prejudices against Muslims and Islam. They and the Russians in fact share the same enmity against Muslims and Islam, as there is a saying, "Non-believers are a united nation". All non-believers are united in their enmity against Allah, just like a proverb in Pashto that says, "All the dogs are united against the poor". Non-believers are united against Muslims and they dreamt of occupying Afghanistan for a long time. The Americans were thinking about it, but did not have the opportunity, because the Russians were near Afghanistan. They did not help Afghan mujahedeen forces against the Russians because they were hurt by the violations of Muslims' rights, or because they respected Afghan culture and traditions. If they did not want to invade against Afghans' religion, tradition and culture, what's the reason for everything that is happening now? They are destroying all of these principles now. They paved the ground for their invasion of Afghanistan during the Taliban's rule. They had made up their minds about this invasion years before, but they did not do what the Russians did; they used some wisdom in coming here. They brought all the countries that had some interest in Afghanistan together, while yet more countries came here because they were under the Americans' influence. Then they carried out their pre-planned invasion.

At the beginning, many innocent Afghans were martyred, especially Taliban, who were martyred in heavy bombardments, and many of them were surrendered to Uzbek militias and martyred later on in order to keep the disunity and internal wars going on in the future. It is worth mentioning that a special group of Uzbeks carried out that saddening and savage act; in addition, they imprisoned many people inside and outside the country.

Later on, they frequently bombarded Afghans' traditional gatherings such as weddings, khairats, funerals and other similar gatherings, and turned them to grief. They tested different types of modern weapons that had not been tested yet on Afghans. They conducted night raids in different places; this is still going on. Prisons and detention centres are getting filled with innocent people day by day. Both these non-believing countries invaded Afghanistan, but there are the following differences between their invasions:

1. The cruelty of the communists, which was unlimited, is obvious to both Afghans and foreigners alike. They affected many people and ruined many families. They distributed people's own properties to others. On the other hand, their recruitment was based on communist interests. Although communism was a corrupt, non-Muslim and awkward belief, they had high recruitment, because they wanted to have people as communists to fight for them. Americans and other foreigners on the other hand are inviting people to Christianity and want to find friends in faith. A good example of this is Abdul Rahman, who was given the death penalty for converting to Christianity, but then non-believers took him to Rome, applauded him and gathered great wealth for him for accepting Christianity.
2. The second difference is that the Russians' prisons were very full and there was much cruelty in them. However, American prisons were not as full and they had prisons both inside and outside the country. Clerics, influential people, good and talented people and those who had memorised the Qur'an were in both Russian and American prisons.
3. Although it does not really have much to do with the Americans, administrative corruption was at a lower level during Russian rule. Now it's just overwhelming.
4. The Russians would not disrespect people; they would either kill you or made you suffer in prison. However, the Americans disrespect and dishonour people in different ways; they take pictures of detainees while they are unclothed; they cut dead bodies of people killed in battles in pieces and then take pictures with the body parts, or savagely pee on dead bodies and many more things like this.

5. The Russian military would fight and attack mujahedeen; they would fight in every metre of the land, even though their equipment was weaker and less sophisticated compared to current military equipment. However, the Americans only use their equipment, and their soldiers are without zeal; they cry during battles and just scream instead of fighting.

WHAT IS A 'TERRORIST'?

It is amazing that yesterday when I benefited them, I was considered the hero of freedom and independence, but today, now that I have stood against them, I am considered a terrorist. Afghans fought against the Russians during the jihad for the freedom and independence of their country. At that time, the Americans were the first to help, and considered the mujahedeen to be victors. Our neighbouring country, Pakistan, which Afghans saved from Russian influence with the price of their blood, had given Afghans much freedom, to the extent that Afghan vehicles could travel around in Pakistan without having any documents or registration. All this was just because they wanted to use Afghans as a shield against the big Soviet dragon, and now that they are safe from the big dragon, they've stopped welcoming Afghans. Now that the internationals call those same Afghans terrorists, Pakistan followed the steps of the non-believers and stamped Afghans as terrorists. They killed many Afghans by beating them and torturing them. Many other Afghans have been disabled. It is obvious that Pakistan's past good treatment and hospitality for Afghans was not for the sake of Islam, but for Pakistan's own benefit.

Similarly, when Muslims in any other part of the world are being attacked, they are first named terrorists to create an excuse for beating them up. They martyred millions of Afghans, left millions more with disabilities and forced millions of them to flee from the country for years. They decreased knowledge and culture and ruined Afghanistan's military structure and system. They destroyed years-old orchards and agriculture, but nobody called them terrorists. The US held mass killings in Vietnam and then killed and incarcerated hundreds of thousands of innocent people in Iraq. The dishonouring of Muslim men and women in Abu Ghraib prison was just one example of their behaviour. They did every wrongdoing that possibly comes to mind in Afghanistan. They took innocent people to various detention centres, such as Guantánamo; they bombarded houses and martyred hundreds of women, elders and children; and many more such savage actions that I would not mention here. Despite this, nobody told them that they themselves were the real terrorists. Jews in the blood-thirsty Israel have invaded Palestine and occupied that holy land. Palestinians bravely started fighting them back and are committed to the freedom of their country. This bloody fight is still going on, and hundreds of people are being martyred every day. Still, nobody calls Israel terrorist or invader. It's only the oppressed Muslims who are called terrorists. Israelis who are cruel are free from being called terrorists. Therefore, it is clear that the word terrorist is used for Muslims and weak societies; however, whoever has power and is cruel, especially the Jews and the Christians, could not be called terrorists at all. Whenever the cruel decides to crush the oppressed, they would just attach the terrorist title to the oppressed to use it as a pretext to save themselves from embarrassment.

Pashtuns have an old story that once a wolf was drinking water from a stream and a sheep was drinking water from the same stream, but downstream from the wolf. The water flow was from the wolf towards the sheep; still, the wolf looked for excuses and asked the sheep why she was disturbing the water. The wolf jumped on the sheep with this pretext and then ate her. The current situation is very similar to this story. You make your own judgement and see that all the prisons are filled with oppressed people who are spending time in detention in contradiction to all international standards. Detainees in Guantánamo as well are kept without observation of any international rule or standard. There are many people in Bagram who have not done anything. Pakistan too arrested thousands of citizens of different countries; not only that, but they also tortured the people they arrested in many different ways. I saw many people who had become disabled due to being beaten; they wouldn't hear anything from their families, and nobody was given justice. The treatment in Pakistani detention centres was intolerable. Their treatment did not comply with Islam,

Muslims or humanity. It was hard to spend time there; they would arrest a good Muslim, call him a terrorist and then impose their wrongdoings and oppression on him.

JIHAD AND WHAT FOLLOWED

It is an obvious fact that the Afghans carried out a jihad against the Russians the likes of which cannot be found in recent history. During the Afghans' jihad against the red invaders, not only Muslims and Muslim countries, but also other countries such as America, France, Germany and China, that are opponents of Islam, also helped the Afghans to defeat their enemy, the powerful Soviet Union. The significant point is that all mujahedeen had holy goals at the beginning of jihad. They were doing jihad just for the satisfaction of almighty Allah, the survival of Islam and the freedom of the homeland from the red occupier. Mujahedeen did not pay attention to anything else other than these points and that is how they were able to defeat the infidel superpower with empty hands, hungry stomachs and a small number of very simple weapons. Nobody even considered the possibility of the mujahedeen's victory. The Afghans' victory was miraculous, because overcoming such a powerful and well-equipped army seemed impossible. Most mujahedeen performed jihad just for the sake of Allah as an Islamic duty and expected martyrdom any moment. Afghans tolerated heavy financial and human loss in that war; the entire country was ruined and over two and half million people were martyred. Many mujahedeen were martyred by mines during the war. They would succeed against the red enemy in face to face battles even when they were smaller in number. That was the truth based on a verse from Qur'an, "A small number of people (Muslims) would succeed against the larger number with the order of Allah and Allah is with those who are patient". It is worth mentioning that during the ten-year war of the red invading army, hundreds of thousands of soldiers, thousands of tanks and other military vehicles, and hundreds of war planes came to Pashmol, but they still were not able to defeat a small number of mujahedeen, who were probably not more than a hundred people. In short, the mujahedeen became victorious at the end regardless of what they went through and became an example for mujahedeen in other parts of the world such as Palestine, Chechnya, Uzbekistan, Tajikistan, Turkmenistan, Azerbaijan and many more. Afghans sent them a message of ending oppression and showed them all that independence could be achieved through giving sacrifice and performing jihad. When Karzai's administration was established after the interference of the Bonn Agreement, most power was given to influential Afghans who have come from the West and most mujahedeen were kept away from power. Those communists against whom the mujahedeen had fought for tens of years and who are to blame for all the current problems in the country, were appointed in high positions in most governmental organisations. A good example of this is my stories of when I was in detention. All the power in the National Directorate of Security was in the hands of communists, and mujahedeen like me who had fought the puppet communists were left in their hands. Administrative affairs from investigation and interviewing to beyond were all in the hands of those communists.

THE CURRENT ABUSE OF NARCOTICS COMPARED WITH ALCOHOL IN AFGHANISTAN

Despite the fact that drugs are harmful to society, they harm the brain, make individuals high and are considered *haram*, clerics consider cultivating them permissible. There is *ushr* and *zakat* in them, and if they come into contact with one's clothes, they do not spoil them . Alcohol has been declared *haram* in explicit verses of the holy words of Allah in the Qur'an. I spent almost five years in Afghan prisons and I witnessed that the second most common prisoners after political prisoners were people incarcerated for drug crimes. It is worth mentioning that if you look at character and religious spirituality, the drug offenders came second after political prisoners. There were many of them, and mostly serving long sentences, up to twenty, eighteen, sixteen or twelve years. However, you would not see a single person incarcerated for alcohol. And even if somebody was brought to the detention centre for alcohol related crimes, he would get released very quickly. Despite alcohol use and business being a crime according to Afghan laws, there are no inmates locked for alcohol related crimes in any of the prisons in the country. Many people are plagued with this impermissible disease, but no efforts are made to treat people or lock them up for it. The only reason for this is because the foreigners residing in our country have control over things and do whatever is for the benefit of their countries. As drugs are harmful for their countries, they take serious steps against them, but when it comes to alcohol, they consider it something plain and ignore it. Unfortunately, although our people know that alcohol is *haram*, they do not prevent the use, sale or import of alcohol in order to keep the foreigners happy, regardless of the disrespect to the religion and the law here. If we assume that the current government prevented alcohol use, you would see that the future generation would be rescued from this problem, and the number of prisoners for this crime would be greater than for any other crime, all over the country. May Allah keep our country from non-believers' occupations and their immoral culture and vice. Accept our prayer, Lord of all kingdoms.

Sayyed Mohammad Akbar Agha
The eleventh month of 1390 (January 2012)
Kabul, Afghanistan

Notes

1. Ali Jalali and Lester Grau, The Other Side of the Mountain, p 315
2. Also known as Sayyeds.
3. He was buried in Kulapur, India.
4. His shrine is in Kunar province.
5. He was buried in Sanjawi Tahsil area of Lorlayee Zela.
6. His grave may be found in Auch Sharif of Punjab, Pakistan.
7. He laid the foundation stone of Halima Jami'a of Darabizu in Lakai Marut.
8. He was the Minister of Refugees during the Rabbani government time.
9. The Ministry for the Promotion of Virtue and Suppression of Vice.
10. Snuff.
11. This is the battle fought in 624 by the Prophet Mohammad.
12. During his six-month period of administration, Burhanuddin Rabbani created this council that voted that Rabbani continue to be the president.
13. This refers to the Taliban's treasury.

www.ingramcontent.com/pod-product-compliance
Ingram Content Group UK Ltd.
Pitfield, Milton Keynes, MK11 3LW, UK
UKHW021933190726
13853UKWH00004B/1411

9 783944 214092